Steel-String Guitar Construction

By Irving Sloane

CLASSIC GUITAR CONSTRUCTION
GUITAR REPAIR
STEEL-STRING GUITAR CONSTRUCTION

Acoustic Six-String, Twelve-String and Arched-Top Guitars

STEEL-STRING GUITAR CONSTRUCTION
by Irving Sloane

A Sunrise Book
E. P. DUTTON & CO., INC.
NEW YORK

Copyright © 1975 by Irving Sloane
All rights reserved. Printed in the U.S.A.
Dutton-Sunrise, Inc., a subsidiary of E. P. Dutton & Co., Inc.

10 9 8 7 6 5 4 3 2

Published simultaneously in Canada by Clarke, Irwin & Company Limited, Toronto and Vancouver

ISBN: 0-87690-172-0

Library of Congress Cataloging in Publication Data

Sloane, Irving.
    Steel-string guitar construction.

    "A Sunrise book."
    1. Guitar—Construction. I. Title.
ML1016.G8S66   787'.61'2   75-5890

for Dave, Linda, and Roy

ACKNOWLEDGMENTS

I am indebted to the many busy people who took time out to answer my questions and offer assistance.

Mike Longworth and Earl Remaley of C. F. Martin & Co.; Thomas P. Fetters of Gibson Inc., and retired Gibson executive and archivist, Julius Bellson. Information about strings came from John D'Addario of D'Addario Strings, Walter Watson of National Standard Co. (Worcester Wire Division), and Kenneth Bowen of Wasa Steel.

The lumber sawing pictures were taken at the South Amboy yard of J. H. Monteath Co. In London, Louis Gallo showed me his Maccaferri guitar collection, and another Londoner, Chris Eccleshall, provided detail drawings of Maccaferri construction.

R. Lloyd-Owen of Harris Ivory Works provided an interesting tour.

Most of the decorative instruments in the chapter on fancy work appear through the courtesy of Walter Lipton. James D'Aquisto, an exceptionally busy luthier, endured long hours of photographic interruptions with unfailing grace and humor. My wife, also, bore with patience and understanding many small crises and long periods of sequestered labor.

Alberto Aroldi took the cover photograph and E. I. Weiss contributed valuable photographic assistance.

To all of them I offer my grateful appreciation and sincere thanks.

Irving Sloane

Preface

Until I was fourteen I lived on East Tenth Street in lower Manhattan. A few blocks west lay the Third Avenue district of pawnshops. I used to stand for hours at their windows, gaping at the second-hand cutlery, fishing rods, cameras, accordions, gold rings, tools, mandolins, trumpets, and guitars.

I returned to a Third Avenue pawnshop to buy a guitar with my first earnings as a merchant seaman. My last pawnshop guitar was an f-hole Orpheum.

My sailing career ended in early 1946. I came back to the old neighborhood to see a boyhood friend. In the vestibule of the tenement where his father was janitor, I searched the mailboxes. A nameplate held my attention: "H. Ledbetter— 5A." I quickly climbed the stairs to the top floor and rang the doorbell. "Come in . . . it's open!"

I opened the door. A powerful, graying black man stood in his shorts before an ironing board. He was pressing his pants.

"Are you Leadbelly, the folk singer?"

He smiled and slipped on his pants. "That's me," he said simply, and folded up the ironing board.

We sat and talked about guitars, songs, and his wanderings in the South. He knew a thousand songs. Did he know "Bundle Up 'n Go," a song taught me by a sailor from Alabama?

He grimaced, shaking his head in puzzlement.

"Wait a minute . . . wait a minute . . . you must mean 'Bottle Up 'n Go' . . ." and he was off playing and singing the song.

He was in the twilight of his life and made occasional money playing at private parties for twenty-five dollars a night. His wife, Babe, worked and was their mainstay. During my visits I made no secret of my admiration for Josh White and played my homely imitations of his famous style.

"Hell," Leadbelly said, "Josh often comes here.

Call me up nex' time you come an' I'll get him over here if you're dyin' to meet him."

A few weeks later I called.

"Yeah, he's due here this afternoon," Leadbelly said. "But bring a bottle because he likes to belt 'em."

I showed up with a pint of whisky. We waited and Leadbelly played twelve-string blues. He had an old upright piano, and I shamelessly vamped the bass line of "Panassie Stomp" while he played along, smiling encouragement. The afternoon was waning and no Josh White. Leadbelly poured us a drink.

"Might as well have us a drink while we waitin'."

Josh never came, and soon after I moved to New Jersey. I spoke to Leadbelly on the phone once or twice.

"When you gonna draw my picture?" he asked.

He knew I was an artist, and I had promised to do it but I never did.

From 1949 to 1957 I worked out of a studio on Spring and Lafayette streets, around the corner from D'Angelico's guitar shop on Kenmare Street. At odd hours I watched D'Angelico at work in the window, wrapped in melancholy absorption, gluing endless layers of black and white celluloid binding. Onlookers made him nervous and provoked dark looks.

I thought his guitars were cumbersome and heavy, nothing like the Barbero my teacher played. I was studying flamenco then and was dazzled by the elegance of Santos, Barbero, and Esteso guitars.

I talked to my teacher about the possibility of making a guitar. He groped in a closet and came up with a Barbero neck, all that was left of a guitar smashed by Mario Escudero at Carnegie Hall.

"Take it with you," he said, smiling a sly Spanish smile. "You won't make a guitar . . . for that you have to be Spanish. But, who knows, try."

I did, and I hope you will too.

I. S.

Contents

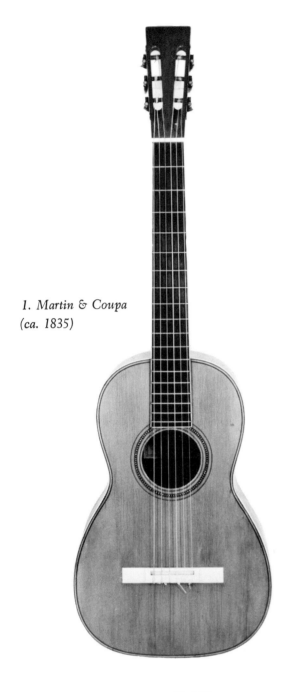

1. *Martin & Coupa*
(*ca. 1835*)

Beginnings

Until after the Civil War, few Americans knew how to read music. Self-taught, instinctive musicianship was the rule. Music without words, based on formal theories of counterpoint and harmony, was in fact unknown to most Americans until the late nineteenth century.

This lack of a tradition rooted in classical European music helped shape the character of American music. Rhythm, the stepchild of classical music, and a strong melodic line became the hallmarks of the folk, hillbilly, and jazz traditions that are uniquely American.

Along with the banjo and mandolin, the guitar fell naturally into the musical scheme. With the mastery of a few simple chords, it could be played in any tempo, slow to fast. The enduring popularity of the guitar is due to its broad range of expression, made possible by a rich variety of playing techniques.

Two men stand out in the history of the commercial development of the guitar in the United States: Christian Frederick Martin and Orville H. Gibson.

Martin arrived in New York from Germany in 1833. He was an experienced guitar maker, having trained and worked in his native Saxony and served as a foreman for the Stauffer instrument works in Vienna. His first venture was a music store on Hudson Street, where he sold a full line of musical instruments, sheet music, strings, and guitars of his own manufacture. Early Martin guitars were gut-strung, had pin bridges, and bore "Martin & Coupa" or "Martin & Schatz" labels. John Coupa was a guitar teacher and also an outlet for Martin's handmade guitars, which appears to be the only reason for his name on the label. Henry Schatz, an old friend from Saxony, evidently built some of the guitars sold during the New York period.

In 1839 Martin moved his family and business to Nazareth, Pennsylvania, and began in earnest the company that continues there today. Freed of the distrac-

2. *Christian Frederick Martin, 1796–1873*

3. *One of the first guitars built by Orville Gibson*

tions of the New York music store, he began to develop his ideas about guitar design and construction. The famous X-brace, an important feature of modern guitar manufacture, was devised by Martin during those first formative years in Nazareth.

C. F. Martin & Company was an established, though modest, enterprise when Orville Gibson was born in Chateaugay, New York, in 1856. Little is known about his early life until the 1880s, when Kalamazoo directories record a gray procession of rooming houses and clerking jobs for an "O. H. Gibson." Finally, an 1896 entry lists "O. H. Gibson, Manufacturer Musical Instruments." Gibson appears to have mysteriously arrived at his chosen career in full-blown possession of formidable gifts for which no special training had prepared him. He had taught himself to make musical instruments.

Gibson was clearly a craftsman of extraordinary skill and was obsessed with the idea of incorporating the principles of violin arching in the construction of

4. *Orville Gibson in flamboyant moment, 1890s*

5. "Dobro" National

mandolins and guitars. He disdained the traditional lute-form mandolin as a "potato bug."

By the 1890s public fervor for the mandolin was so intense that even Martin began making mandolins (lute form), and by the turn of the century the mandolin mania was in full stride. Mandolin orchestras sprouted all over the country and everywhere else in the world. Eager players rushed to buy mandolins, mandolas, mando-cellos, mando-basses, guitars, harp-guitars, and tenor guitars. Virtuoso mandolin performers were lionized by the public, and the music trade press was filled with exhilarating news of fresh commercial triumphs.

In 1902 Orville Gibson sold his instrument-making skills, inventions, and name to a group of five Kalamazoo businessmen. In an agreement patently devised to preclude long-term involvement, Gibson agreed to supervise for two years the design and construction of musical instruments to be sold by the Gibson Mandolin-Guitar Manufacturing Company. The new company prospered, and after his agreement was fulfilled, Gibson's official association with the company appears to have dwindled to that of informal consultant. Failing health, reportedly, obliged him to leave Kalamazoo, and he died in Ogdensburg, New York, in 1918.

A change in musical fashion after World War I signaled the end of the mandolin. The four-square musical rhythms of the flapper era were beginning to take hold, and soon the banjo was incontestable king. Gibson went into banjo manufacture in a big way, and another fad, the ukulele craze of the 1920s, gave C. F. Martin & Company a period of dynamic growth. All this time the guitar seems to have been gaining a steady foothold in both orchestral and small group work. In the late twenties a hillbilly group called the Skillet Lickers, led by blind guitarist Riley Puckett, was in the fore of a surging interest in country music. Jazz was beginning to command a wider audience, and the big swing bands came into being, cresting the wave of the public's new enthusiasm for ballroom dancing. And all this had the powerful impetus of a new medium, radio.

The twenties also saw the appearance of innovation in guitar construction. A metal guitar featuring resonators was patented by the Dopera brothers, a straightforward attempt to cash in on the fantastic success of the banjo by providing a guitar with the brassy timbre of the banjo. Today, the Dobro is more popular than ever, unlike another such attempt, the Cremona guitar-banjo, which was a Gibson-type guitar with a banjo resonator built into the center of the soundboard.

In 1927 a young Italian concert guitarist-builder, Mario Maccaferri, produced an unusual guitar. It held a separate sound chamber within the guitar sound box. On a principle similar to that used in the bass reflex cabinet, an inner sound chamber was formed by a false bottom positioned about an inch above the back. Laminated hardwood sides set back from the outer sides enclosed this inner chamber. A hole or port in the upper end of this sound chamber opened onto a

(Photo: Mel Lewis)

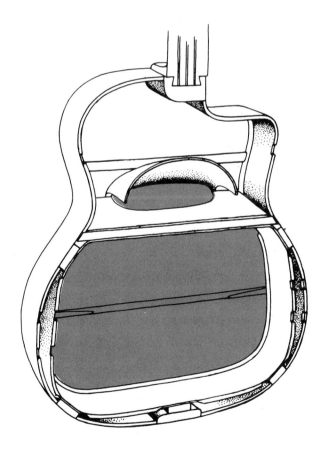

6. *Interior view of steel-string "D" sound hole Maccaferri*

curved deflector directly under the sound hole. The Maccaferri guitar of this type was noted for its brilliant tone and loudness and was the favored instrument of the great Belgian gypsy guitarist, Django Reinhardt.

The swing era saw the emergence of a new kind of guitar player, a sophisticated stylist who broadened

11

the expressive range of the guitar to include single-string and chord styles new to the instrument. Eddie Lang, Teddy Bunn, Charlie Christian, Jimmy Shirley, and Django Reinhardt were among the important players of that era.

After World War II, interest in the guitar began to build and by the early 1960s exploded into a national passion for all kinds of guitars. The passion shows no signs of abating. Today a growing interest in guitars is found in countries around the world as the explosion continues its outward momentum.

Unlike the classic guitar, which has until recently been exclusively in the hands of custom luthiers, the steel-string guitar has from its inception been an item of commercial manufacture. Competitive pressures tend to weight innovation heavily on the side of streamlining production and product uniformity. In some degree, of course, these concerns govern the efforts of anyone who is in the marketplace, including custom luthiers. But the dedicated amateur is free of these restraints. He or she can experiment, risk failure, and try something else. The great guitars waiting to be built may come from a small back-room workshop like the one Orville Gibson had.

7. *Gibson L-4, 1926 (neck and fretboard not original)*

8. *Orville Gibson's workshop*

Strings

The drawing of metal wire suitable for stringing musical instruments dates from about A.D. 1350 at Nuremberg, Germany. A thick rod of malleable metal—brass and later steel—was tapered at one end so it could be led through a hole smaller than its own diameter. The end was gripped with stout pliers and pulled through the drawplate made of a harder metal. Drawing the rod through successively smaller holes produced thin wires of varying gauges.

Gut and silk strings were in use since ancient times, but lacked the advantages of metal strings which seldom broke and stayed in tune when the instrument was idle or played under a hot sun. However, gut strings made from sheep intestines were common until the advent of nylon strings. Silk was used for the finest-gauge strings but more often served as a core for overspun strings.

Overwrapping a silk or gut core is believed to have been introduced in France during the seventeenth century. Spurred by the availability of drawn wire, the clavichord and harpsichord were developing rapidly, and the need for deeper tunings brought about the overspun string. Wrapping a wire over a core string increases its mass, thereby lowering its vibrating pitch.

Modern strings use a core wire of steel with a trace of nickel content. The wire is drawn through a series of dies and annealed at various stages to facilitate drawing. Core wires—formerly round—are now drawn in hexagonal and octagonal shapes to simplify string manufacture. An overspun wire on such a core will not unravel if the string is cut, a benefit for player as well as manufacturer. Wires used for overwrapping include bronze, silvered copper, stainless steel, nickel, brass, and zinc-covered low-carbon steel.

Compound strings use a core of steel with nylon, silk, or rayon. They are wound with silver-plated wire and combine a less metallic sound with light-gauge tension. Flat-wound strings use a flat overwrapped wire and have the advantage of a smooth feel with minimal finger squeak caused by glissando. Their sound is more subdued than round-wound strings, and they go dead more quickly.

9. Fifteenth-century wire-drawer sat in a swing to permit use of feet for leverage

Overwrapping is done on an automatic winding machine. The core string is stretched taut between two hooks that revolve at high speed while a moving arm feeds the overwrap wire onto the spinning core. For hand-wound strings a trained operator substitutes for the machine's moving arm. Paradoxically, hand-wound strings are supposed to be more uniform than those made by machine.

Poor intonation, falseness, and lack of brilliance are common symptoms of a bad string. Perspiration, grease, tarnish, and dirt all take their corrosive toll. Changes in the string diameter caused by overstretching, fret denting, and hard use of a pick affect the vibrating character of a string. String buzz can sometimes be traced to a nut groove. If the string is not cleanly stopped at the front face of the nut, it will rattle in the groove and make a buzzing sound.

Efforts to preserve strings in the face of normal wear and tear are largely futile. Wiping the strings with a clean cotton cloth after playing is a good idea, especially if your fingers perspire. And a string's newness is no guarantee of smooth sailing. New strings that give poor intonation because of manufacturing flaws are by no means rare.

A string is secured by lodging the ball end against the reinforcing plate under the bridge. The taper of the pinhole is designed to secure the pin and not the string. Besides the risk of cracking the bridge, continually forcing in the pin will eventually enlarge the hole to the point where the wedging action is lost. When this happens, a new, thicker set of pins must be fitted to the enlarged holes.

10. Wire being drawn through successively smaller dies

(*Wasa Steel*)

11. String winding machine

Construction Theory

The volume of sound produced by a guitar depends to a great extent on the volume of air enclosed by the resonating sound cavity or box. Large, deep boxes produce a louder sound and give a deeper bass response than small, shallow boxes, which tend toward the treble end of the scale and suffer a proportional reduction in volume or loudness.

Sound is produced by plucking a string whose vibrations move the air that surrounds the string. This vibrating air in turn communicates these vibrations to the large extended surface of the soundboard. String vibrations are also transmitted to the soundboard through the bridge. The resultant ultrarapid rise and fall of the resonating diaphragm (soundboard) set air in motion inside the sound chest, amplifying and increasing the duration of sound waves. This amplitude is what gives body and power to the tone of a guitar.

In the traditional construction of a classic guitar, great importance is attached to the character and disposition of soundboard bracing. Bracing patterns are

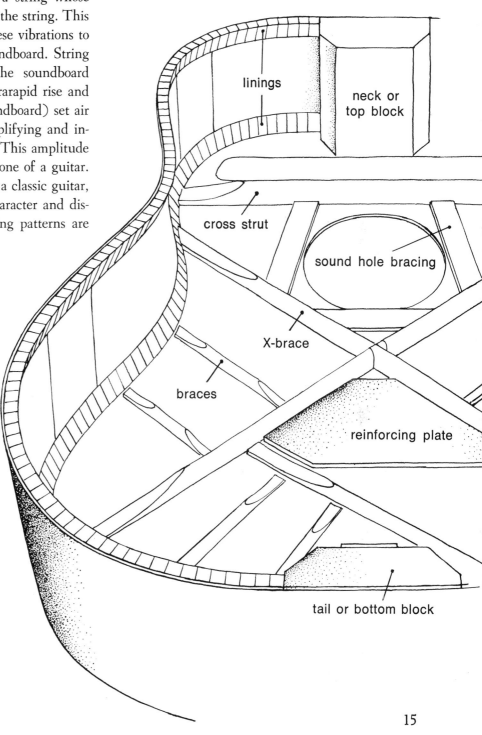

linings

neck or top block

cross strut

sound hole bracing

X-brace

braces

reinforcing plate

tail or bottom block

designed to promote the flow of sound vibrations across the diaphragm like the effect of a stone dropped in the center of a pond; concentric circles of sound vibrations ripple out from the bridge, meeting less and less resistance as they reach the diaphragm perimeter.

The classic guitar is strung with nylon and undergoes much less tension on the bridge than a steel-string guitar. Because of this, makers of steel-string guitars think of bracing first as structural reinforcement and only secondly as acoustic support. This is only as it should be, since no one wants a guitar that is going to fall apart two weeks after it is bought.

The best commercial manufacturers work to fairly close tolerances on this structural/acoustic compromise. They shade toward the acoustic end, not wanting to forfeit sound quality—an important sales advantage— which more massive bracing might imperil. Manufacturers of cheaper guitars use very heavy bracing without regard for sound quality.

A properly constructed guitar has a vibrant, well-braced body and a soundboard especially designed to vibrate. A top that cannot vibrate produces a muffled, insubstantial sound.

A guitar made with a thin back and sides tends to be louder than a guitar made of thicker wood. But a thin guitar also produces disturbing overtones and dissonances unless securely and strategically braced.

The guitar maker's basic job, then, is to build a sound box enclosing an adequate volume of air within walls thin enough to ensure sufficient loudness yet stable enough to preclude harmonic difficulties and with a top that will flex properly to lend body and presence to the sound.

This is a brief description of what the rest of this book will try to document in careful, illustrated detail. The new technique described here is the simplest, least expensive method for building a fine guitar. When you have finished reading *Steel-String Guitar Construction* you should have a broad understanding of the many considerations and judgments that go into the construction of a guitar and a sense of the underlying mystery that animates every luthier in the subtle pursuit of his craft.

Wood

Guitars are made from exotic, precious woods gathered from distant places—rosewood from Brazil or East India, ebony from Africa, spruce from Central Europe or the American and Canadian Northwest, mahogany from Central America. Flamenco guitars are traditionally made of Spanish cypress.

A recurring item in the music trade journals of the early 1900s was the piano manufacturer's lament over the "scarcity and difficulty of obtaining Brazilian rosewood." Seventy years later the situation remains unchanged; Brazilian rosewood is still scarce. Commercial guitar manufacturers have all switched to Indian rosewood, and the chance of their going back to Brazilian rosewood is exceedingly dim.

In an effort to build up its own lumber industry, the Brazilian government has placed an embargo on the export of unfinished logs. Only boards or processed lumber may be shipped abroad. The continuing strong demand for Brazilian rosewood by furniture manufacturers in Scandinavia and Europe makes it unlikely that the Brazilian government will rescind the embargo.

Several factors have made rosewood the guitar wood par excellence. Its exceptional strength and density permit thinness without sacrificing rigidity, and its high resin content gives it superior resistance to decay and warp. Finally, its lustrous, dark-grained beauty is a prized asset in an instrument where visual appearance is an important consideration.

Brazilian rosewood ranges in color from pale red-brown to deep chocolate. Grain is often wild, with pores that can be large or small. The first scraping or planing will reveal a waxy luster and a distinctive resiny fragrance.

Indian rosewood has a more uniform grain and a color ranging from pale gray-brown to deep red-brown or sepia with a vaguely purple haze. Grain is more open-pored than Brazilian and luster is duller. Rough-sawn rosewood, incidentally, appears deceptively lighter in color than finished wood.

In selecting rosewood, avoid—if possible—wood with such obvious defects as cracks, knots, pinholes, black pitch markings, and unsightly color variations. The two pieces for the sides should be perfectly flat and cut in sequence from the same flitch (the original squared-off beam) so ·that grain configuration is almost identical. Avoid boards that are out of wind—twisted diagonally along their length. They will not be straightened by the bending process.

Both halves of the back should also be cut from consecutive pieces of a flitch so that they make a symmetrical design when opened like a book. If back and sides are a close match in both color and grain characteristics, they need not come from the same flitch.

Maple, mahogany, walnut, sepele, and other woods have also been used to make guitars. Rosewood-veneered plywood is also available for backs and sides. Plywood guitars are disappointing, especially if the top is plywood too. But this may be due in part to the general cheapness of their manufacture. The situation might be helped if the wood was two-ply instead of three-ply. It might be less rigid and permit tapering or thinning if necessary.

Soundboards are made of spruce, an even-grained, resonant wood that combines exceptional strength with lightness.

The Tyrol, Dalmatia, the forests of Bohemia and Rumania provided the spruce for generations of European luthiers and are now largely exhausted. Imported spruce is difficult to find and expensive. Two new sources of wood have now gained wide acceptance: Sitka spruce and western red cedar.

Sitka spruce is a large tree growing in the American Northwest, western Canada, and Alaska. Its strength/weight ratio is lower than that of European spruce, but in all other respects it is a perfectly satisfactory replacement. Sapwood is creamy white, with heartwood that shades off to a pale pink. Trees of very large girth are cut and supply almost all of the quartersawn spruce tops used by American guitar manufacturers. Western red cedar, a soft aromatic

13. Sitka spruce log being cut in half, separated with fork lift, and rough cut for band sawing

wood, is now being used for soundboards by some classic guitar builders, but is a poor choice for steel-string guitar construction. Its low inherent strength is against it; a misdirected pick will abrade and scar this soft-fibered wood.

No evidence has come down to us from luthiers of the past that wood was stored for extraordinary lengths of time or that wood a hundred years old is acoustically superior to wood five years old. The chief advantage of using old wood is that it may easily be better than what is generally available today—closer and more evenly grained, of better temper, and perhaps cut more directly on the quarter. Lutherie, like other traditional arts, has its share of tired shibboleths, the best known one being the caution about using ancient wood.

Indian rosewood logs are hauled from the forest by elephant and tractor, loaded on trains, and shipped to the port of embarkation. Freighters bring the logs to their destination, where trucks carry them to the sawmill.

The logs are carefully studied and marked off for sawing that will reduce the log to flitches that will yield boards cut on the quarter. Rosewood logs are usually cut up into flitches on an enormous band saw. The flitches are then locked into place on a long, movable carriage and fed into a 36″ veneer saw that quartersaws the wood into ⅛″ veneers.

There is considerable hazard in cutting rosewood. The sawyer must be constantly on the lookout for signs of a pitch pocket, a cavity lined with a flint-hard mineral encrustation that can shatter a saw blade. When a pocket is encountered, the saw is stopped and the sawyer must cut out the pocket with chisel and sledgehammer. The band sawyer is not so lucky. He cannot see the pockets when the first flitch cutting is done. When the band saw hits a pocket, it's every man for himself.

Sitka spruce logs often have a 5′ or 6′ diameter and trunks are cut into manageable sections of 9′ or 10′ lengths. Rough cutting of the log is done with a chain saw, and the rough flitches are squared off on the big band saw. They are then resawn on the veneer saw,

14. *Slicing mahogany on veneer saw*

A cross section of a tree shows the following well-defined features: bark, divided into the outer, corky dead part and the thin, inner, living part; cambium layer (microscopic), lying next to inner bark and responsible for forming wood and bark cells; sapwood, which contains living cells and has an active role in the life processes of the tree, carrying sap from roots to leaves; heartwood, usually the major portion of a log, composed of inactive cells formed by changes in the living cells of the inner sapwood rings; pith, a small central core of soft tissue about which the first wood growth takes place; wood rays, connecting the various layers in a radiating pattern from pith to bark for storage and transfer of food.

Growth rings tell the age of a tree and produce a parallel linear pattern in sawn lumber referred to as grain. The inner, lighter part of the growth ring is called springwood or early wood, and the outer, darker portion of the ring is called summerwood. Springwood is characterized by cells with relatively large cavities and thin walls. Summerwood cells have smaller cavities and thicker walls. Instrument makers have traditionally sought spruce growing high up near the timberline because the short growing season produces tighter grained, stronger soundboard wood. Contrary to popular belief, moisture content changes very little from season to season.

the same as the rosewood. The sliced veneers are carefully kept in their natural sequence in the flitch.

Soundboards are selected by grain, temper (resilience), and resonance. A good top is seasoned, unblemished, and close-grained. Annular divisions should run between fourteen and twenty per inch. Where the grain widens at the outer edges, the increase should be gradual. End grain should be vertical, ideally, because if it is badly slanted (more than 45°) it means the wood was slab cut and is more likely to warp. A characteristic of the best spruce tone wood is a cross-grained "silk" pattern observable on the finest guitars. This phenomenon is caused by cross-section exposure of the wood rays and is most pronounced when the wood is cut directly on the quarter.

Flexing the board will reveal its resilience. It should be fairly stiff, with only a slight amount of give. Generally, a stiffer board produces a brighter sound than a softer, more flexible board. A very soft, rubbery board that bends easily is not used.

Although the most reliable index for selecting a top is visual, the resonating quality may be judged by lightly grasping the upper edge of one of the halves and gently rapping it with the knuckles of the free hand. Even an inexperienced person can detect differences in resonance by listening carefully. A good, dry soundboard has a certain "live" tone, while a poor one has a relatively dead response. As the wood is worked to the appropriate thinness, thumping produces a brighter, more noticeable ring.

Fingerboards are made of ebony or rosewood. Ebony is always preferred on guitars of high quality because of its durability and lack of grain, and because of the elegant contrast it makes with nickel-silver frets. Jet-black ebony is almost impossible to find; streaks or veinings of gray are common. If these marks are unobtrusive, they will eventually disappear, darkened by the oil and perspiration of the player's hand. If they are prominent enough to require staining, a black stain from Germany (Ebonholzbeize) works well. Both ends of an ebony fingerboard usually come sealed with paraffin or shellac to keep moisture from seeping into the end grain and warping the board. A warped fingerboard that cannot be leveled by planing must be discarded.

Soundboard struts and bracing are made of straight-grained, clear spruce, the stiffer the better. Honduras mahogany is used for the cross struts on a rosewood back, Sitka spruce or maple on a maple back.

Necks are usually made from straight-grained Honduras mahogany, a strong, exceptionally stable wood that ranges in color from beige to a reddish tan. Texture is mellow and easily worked. Excellent necks can also be made from maple, both plain and curly, and from black cherry. Both these woods are heavier and stronger than Honduras mahogany and more difficult to work, but finish more beautifully.

Linings are usually basswood (linden) or mahogany. Bridges are fashioned from a billet of straight-grained rosewood or ebony and are also sold ready-made by supply houses.

List of Materials

Soundboard: 2 pieces spruce 8″ × 20″

Back: 2 pieces rosewood (or other) 8″ × 20″

Sides: 2 pieces rosewood (or other) 5″ × 32″

Neck: block of Honduras mahogany 3″ × 5″ × 24″ or 1″ × 3″ × 36″ for laminated neck; veneer head facing 4″ × 8″

Neck and tail blocks: mahogany 1⅜″ × 4″ × 8″

Neck rod: metal reinforcing rod 15″

Linings: 4 pieces shaped for kerfing 5/16″ × ⅝″ × 30″

Cross struts and braces: quarter sawn Sitka spruce 1″ × 6″ × 24″ will provide enough for top and back

Cross-grain back strip: mahogany 1/16″ × ¾″ × 16″

Bridge: 5/16″ × 1 5/16″ × 8″ (rosewood or ebony)

Fretboard: ebony or rosewood ¼″ × 2¾″ × 18½″

Bridge saddle and nut: ivory or bone

Inlay for back: veneer strip 20″

Purfling: plastic or wood strips 5/16″ × 36″ (buy extras for safety)

Tuning machines: 1 set with screws

Nickel silver fret wire: 52″

15. *Sitka log of large girth*

16. *Guitar wood stacked for shipment*

Humidity and Wood Stability

17. *Guitar wood stacked with spacers for breathing*

Dampness is the enemy of all stringed instruments, particularly the guitar.

If dampness enters wood, the wood swells. In a drier environment the moisture leaves the wood and the wood shrinks to its former size. This cycle of dampness and drying is fairly normal, and a guitar can tolerate these changes if they are gradual and not extreme.

A guitar built in an atmosphere where the relative humidity level is about 65% most of the time will survive well in that atmosphere. If it is removed abruptly to a relative humidity level of 20%, it will surely crack after enough moisture has been lost. If a guitar is built at a humidity level of 35%, acclimated to a 65% humidity level, and then removed to a humidity situation of 20%, it may still crack—but the probability is greatly reduced.

Ideally, a guitar should be built in an atmosphere containing less moisture than the atmosphere in which it will most commonly be used because swelling—the absorption of atmospheric moisture—is a less serious hazard than shrinkage.

The critical surfaces for expansion and contraction in a guitar are the top and back. The end grain—easiest point of entry for atmospheric moisture—is sealed off by the purfling. Absorption of moisture is further retarded by the varnish or other protective finish. If the guitar has been carefully made and properly braced, the problem of swelling is not great. The most scrupulous craftsmanship, however, will count for little in the face of an abrupt, serious loss of moisture and the resultant deformation of wood. Sudden drying out of wooden instruments is the major cause of cracks and seam separation.

Before proceeding with plans to build a guitar, try to find out from your local weather bureau the mean annual average relative humidity for your locality. If it is 53.5%, it would be best to assemble your guitar in an atmosphere that does not exceed this humidity level.

Work in a basement workshop must be done only when the basement is dry—usually during winter months when the furnace dries the air. To extend the working season into the warmer, more humid months, the air in the workshop must be dehumidified. This can be accomplished with an electric dehumidifier, an automatic device that condenses moisture from the atmosphere. An air conditioner also helps control humidity.

If you have been lucky enough to find Brazilian rosewood for your guitar, do not attempt to remove the resin by washing the wood in acetone or any other powerful solvent. The resin content of Brazilian rosewood, an important natural attribute, is responsible for its superior resistance to warp and decay. As far as tone is concerned, the greatest guitars the world has seen have been made from rosewood with the resin content intact. It is reasonable to assume that the makers of these instruments would have removed this resin if they felt it was a tonal liability, and my own belief is that the resin content is a tonal asset.

Unless you are planning a trip down the Snake River in your guitar, do not attempt to waterproof it with compounds sold for such purposes. Pentachlorophenol and copper naphthenate solutions were developed for the preservation of wood exposed to weather and vulnerable to fungus or termite damage. The petroleum oils used in these formulations will not improve dimensional stability and may interfere with the proper drying of lacquer or varnish.

Polyethylene glycol (PEG) is a wood-impregnating compound designed to promote dimensional stability, but it will not inhibit the absorption of moisture. In fact, it is more hygroscopic than wood, but will not itself swell appreciably through the absorption of moisture. For this principle to work, thorough impregnation is necessary, and this will interfere with the adhesion of shellac, lacquer, and some varnishes.

No finish or coating material known will prevent the movement of moisture into and out of wood with variations in atmospheric humidity. And under no circumstance should the interior of a guitar be coated with shellac, lacquer, or other finish in an attempt to defeat this inexorable process. Far better to hazard a crack—a concomitant risk in all wood products—than to permanently flaw the vibratory and resonant character of a guitar.

A good hygrometer—a device for measuring percentage of relative humidity—is an important workshop investment. Hang it on a wall away from doors or windows.

Freshly purchased wood should be kept under a weighted board until acclimated to workshop atmosphere, normally a week or two. After the wood reaches equilibrium with the surrounding atmosphere, it may be stacked on a high shelf and turned over at intervals.

Guitars—complete or incomplete—must never be stored near sources of heat or moisture. Never leave a guitar in a closed case where the sun's rays can cook it, and if you leave your guitar at home during summer vacations, loosen strings and store it in the coolest, driest part of the house. If your case has no protective foam padding, beware of sudden, extreme variations in temperature (going from a heated room out into freezing weather) because rosewood may crack.

Keep in mind always that a guitar, after all, is a relatively fragile, taut ensemble of wood and strings.

18. *Hygrometer*

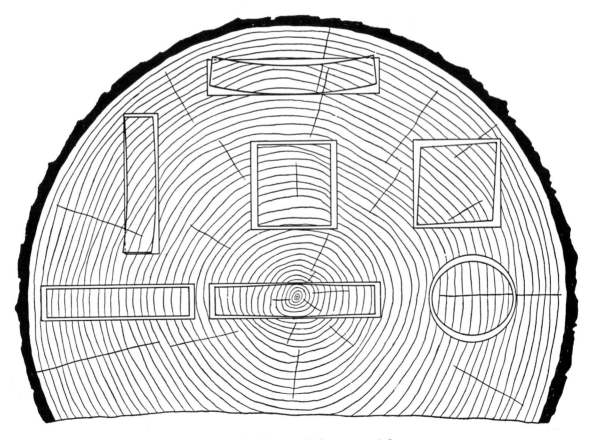

19. *Characteristic shrinkage and distortion of flats, squares, and rounds as affected by the direction of annual rings*

Glue

Several kinds of glue are used in guitar making, each possessing properties that makes it valuable for certain purposes. Considerations that affect the choice of glue include (1) strength requirements, (2) speed of set, (3) water solubility, and (4) solvent resistance.

Titebond (Franklin Glue Co.), a cream-colored aliphatic resin glue, is the glue principally recommended in this book. It is much stronger than polyvinyl resin emulsion glue (Elmer's Glue) and has a built-in tack for a fast initial grabbing action. A high solids content gives it excellent gap-filling ability, an important property in a glue for end-grain joints. Old-time cabinetmakers used to scorch hide glue onto end-grain joints to seal them before attempting to glue them. Titebond dries to a hard film of creamy translucence resistant to lacquer and varnish solvents. It sands well and cures rapidly with a short clamping time.

Polyvinyl resin glue also cures quickly—twenty to thirty minutes at 70° F. It is a white glue that dries transparent and is quite strong. At temperatures below 60° F, the glue turns chalky and strength is impaired. Polyvinyl resin glue is more water soluble than aliphatic resin glue and is used for the tenon joint that joins the neck to the body. If the neck ever needs to be removed for repair, white glue can easily be softened with hot water.

Aliphatic and polyvinyl resin glues have a shelf life of six to eight months and must then be replaced.

Transparent epoxy cement comes in two tubes, one a resin and the other a catalyst or hardener. The two are mixed in equal parts and applied in a thin coating to each gluing surface. Curing time is overnight, and the result is a permanent bond of unequaled strength. Epoxy is a non-water-based glue, is resistant to solvents, and dries clear. All these properties make it a good choice for gluing the center joints of top and back.

Plastic bindings present special problems because plastics are usually bonded by softening their surface to a gluing consistency with the appropriate solvent. For cellulose nitrate plastics, a good glue can be made by chipping up pieces of the plastic (white) and dissolving them in acetone until a thickened consistency is obtained. Plastics of uncertain composition that are insoluble in acetone or other solvent (plastics dealers sometimes sell acetate, acrylic, and other plastic solvents) can be glued with 3M Scotch Super Strength adhesive, although it is somewhat awkward to use because of its gelatinous consistency. Precoating with contact cement will render plastics amenable to use with aliphatic and polyvinyl glues. Scarifying the plastic surface with sandpaper may also permit adhesion with Titebond, but should be tested first.

Cellulose nitrate compounds are dangerously flammable, and all scraps and shavings should be immediately disposed of. Acetone, the principal ingredient of many commercial paint removers, is a comparatively safe material so far as odor and toxicity are concerned. Precautions must be observed regarding its flammability. Its extremely low flash point (−18° C) occurs far below its freezing point.

Hide glue or animal glue made from hooves, bones, sinews, and skin linings of cattle has been the staple adhesive of lutherie for hundreds of years. This glue is manufactured in grades of varying strength and comes in sheet, flake, or granular form. Animal glue is prepared by placing the glue in a double-jacket gluepot with enough water to cover and leaving it to soak. When the glue has absorbed as much water as it can hold, the gluepot is heated to a temperature that should not exceed 140° F. Excessive heat destroys the strength of the glue, repeated heating weakens and thickens it; more water must then be added, further weakening the glue.

The best grades of hide glue are strong and dependable. For optimum results the glue must be freshly made to the right consistency and temperature. Gluing is done quickly in a warm room so that clamps can be applied before the glue jells. Liquid hide glue also comes in ready-to-use form. It has many of the same qualities of hot glue without the elaborate preparations. Setting time is slower, permitting ample time for coating and assembly before clamping.

Animal glues have the advantage of facilitating removal of the plates (top and back) for repairs. A hot knife and carefully applied moisture will separate a glued joint—an advantage more meaningful for violins than guitars, since many repairs can be made to a guitar through the sound hole. The chief drawback of animal glue is that it draws moisture from the atmosphere; exposure to repeated cycles of dampness and drying eventually weakens the glue. In the old days, glue failure was a common cause of frequent repair.

Gluing is best accomplished by having both gluing surfaces perfectly smooth. Tests conducted by the U.S. Department of Agriculture's forest products laboratory showed that no benefit derives from intentional roughening of gluing surfaces. In fact, if the gluing surfaces could be smoothed so perfectly that a thin, even glue line could be produced, no clamping pressure would be required. As a practical matter this almost never occurs, and clamping pressure must be used. Clamps bring the gluing surfaces in close enough contact to produce a thin, uniform glue line and hold them in this position until the glue develops enough strength to hold them together.

Good gluing practice requires application of glue to both surfaces to be glued. If only one surface is covered and makes a spotty transfer of glue to the other surface, a starved joint may result. The glue will penetrate into the wood of each surface leaving insufficient glue for the uniform glue line essential to a good joint.

If surfaces are planed or sanded too soon after gluing with a water-based glue, a sunken joint may result. The water in the glue swells the wood surrounding the glue joint; if the wood is smoothed immediately after gluing, the joint will shrink when the moisture finally leaves.

On resinous wood, such as Brazilian rosewood, a better joint will result if the rosewood gluing area is cleaned with a rag soaked in acetone, benzol, or toluol. It is necessary to clean only the surface of free resin or waxiness.

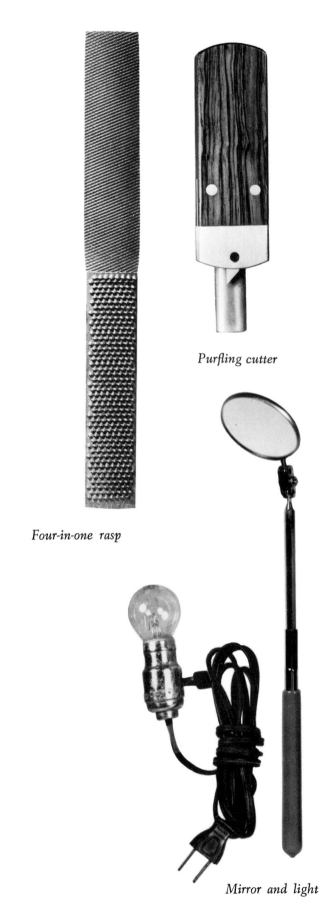

Purfling cutter

Four-in-one rasp

Mirror and light

Tools

Deep-throat clamps and a purfling cutter are the only unusual tools used in guitar making (except for a round-bottom plane used to carve arched-top guitars). Simple plans for making these tools are described elsewhere in this book. In addition, these ordinary tools are needed:

Fine backsaw or dovetail saw
Medium-size backsaw for cutting fret grooves
Jigsaw or coping saw
½" and 1" gouges
¼", ½", and ¾" chisels
Scraper blades and burnisher
Hand scrapers
Adjustable block plane
Hand or power drill with ⁵⁄₁₆" and ⅜" bits
Assorted clamps
Metal straightedge
Light and inspection mirror

If you own power tools—radial or bench saw, jigsaw, router, band saw, and drill press—you will save time, but a fine guitar can be made without any power equipment.

Cutting tools must be kept at razor sharpness for maximum working efficiency. Sharp tools are a pleasure to use and safer than dull ones. More force is necessary to use a dull tool, making a slip more likely; and a dull tool can cut you just as badly as a sharp one. If you have never worked with a really sharp chisel, the experience will be a revelation to you. Chisels are important tools in instrument making.

A combination India stone (aluminum oxide) with medium and fine-grit surfaces will do a good job of basic sharpening. For a surgical cutting edge a Hard Arkansas stone is necessary.

Lubricate the stone with Bear Oil or 3-in-One oil mixed with a little kerosene. The fluid floats away metal and abrasive particles that might otherwise clog the stone. Hold the cutting bevel of the tool against the stone and hone with a small circular motion. It is easier to control an orbital motion than a long, sweeping motion that is likely to rock the bevel. When

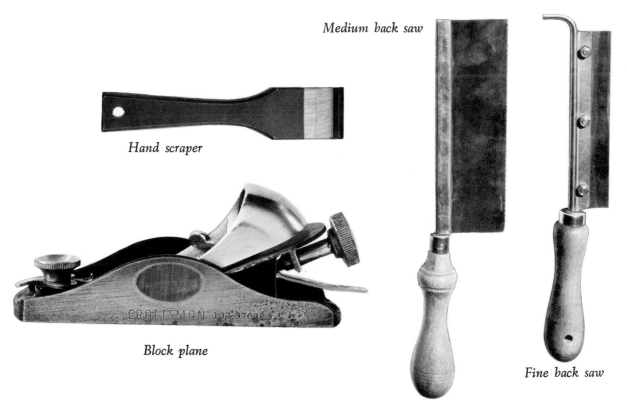

Medium back saw

Hand scraper

Block plane

Fine back saw

20. Tools used in guitar making

the bevel is as sharp as you can get it on the fine India stone, switch to the Hard Arkansas stone. Hone until all scratches are gone, leaving the bevel shiny-smooth. Turn the blade over and hold it flat against the stone. Remove the wire edge by moving the blade sideways about an inch. If the edge is properly sharpened, it will easily shave hair from the back of your hand. Repeat the fine honing until it does.

Gouges are sharpened with a sweeping, rolling motion as they are passed over the stone. The burr on the inner edge is removed with a wedge-shaped round-nosed slipstone.

Cabinet scraper blades, when they are edged correctly, will remove a decent-sized shaving. Their principal virtue is that they do not round edges the way sandpaper does. Among Japanese cabinetmakers the use of sandpaper is considered an abomination; they do all fine shaving of wood with a scraper blade. A scraper blade produces a clean, fuzz-free surface that cannot be duplicated with sandpaper.

Drawing an edge on a steel scraper blade is a tricky job that requires some practice. The long edges must be honed dead flat and square by sliding the blade over the stone using a wooden support to keep it perfectly vertical. The blade is then laid on its side and honed until the edge is knife-edge square. Position the blade on the edge of the workbench and draw a steel burnisher across the flat face of the blade along the edge. Do this once or twice to draw the edge, which you then turn over, by holding the burnisher upright and running it across the edge at a slight angle. Oil the edge before burnishing.

The best way of avoiding the rounding of edges with sandpaper is to make sanding sticks. Glue strips of sandpaper to both sides of a wooden stick about ⅜" × 1¾" × 18". Sticks can be covered with fresh sandpaper and reused.

21. *Polished end of file used as burnisher*

22. *After drawing the edge, it is turned over into a long cutting burr*

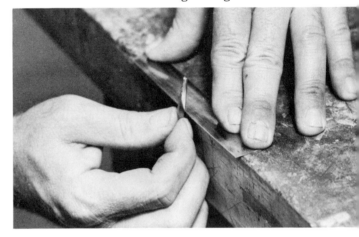

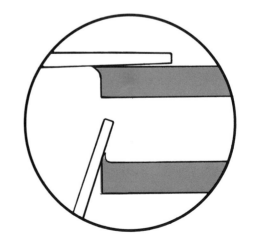

Guitar Maker's Clamps

A deep-throat clamp, a useful guitar-making tool, is easy to make. Its quick flip action makes it convenient for long-reach clamping of braces and for temporary holding jobs. On a guitar with twelve frets clear of the body, it fits through the sound hole for clamping the bridge. It is not intended for heavy clamping pressure, but gives adequate pressure for most guitar gluing jobs. This is an adaptation of a commercially available imported clamp; its advantage is that the jaws are offset so they will clear interior struts when used for clamping the bridge.

The clamp has a fixed lower and a movable upper jaw. When the clamp is fastened about an object, raising the lever brings pressure to bear. Pressure is released by flipping the lever down. The upper jaw can then be raised clear by gripping it just behind the aluminum shaft and pulling up.

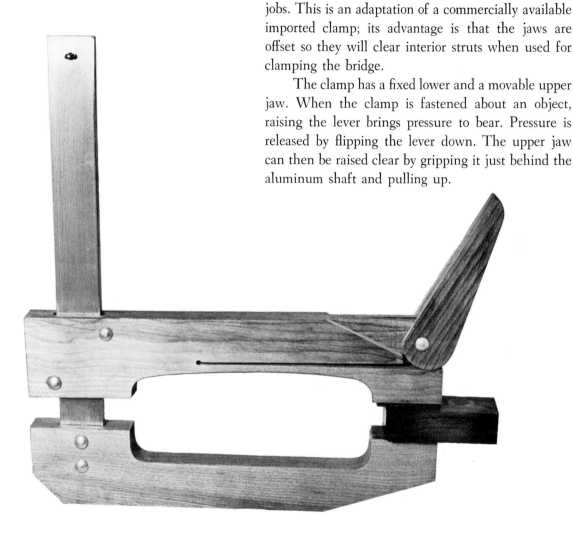

23. Flipping lever up applies pressure

A $1^{3}\!/_{16}'' \times 3^{3}\!/_{4}'' \times 48''$ length of birch will make four clamps and leave enough to make a purfling cutter. You also need a $^{1}\!/_{4}'' \times 1''$ aluminum bar strip (sold in 6' lengths at hardware stores), two dozen 1'' rivets with recessed ends that can be peened over, plus four $^{1}\!/_{2}''$ cotter pins.

Lay out the pattern and saw off the end with the

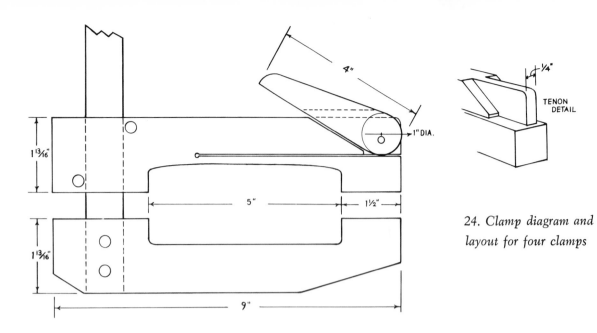

24. Clamp diagram and layout for four clamps

levers drawn on it. Rip down the center of the long remaining piece. Cut off each set of jaws. Mark on each jaw the oblong mortise where the aluminum shaft goes. Drill a series of ¼″ holes in each mortise and chisel through. When the slots are cleared, smooth the inner walls with a flat file.

Cut off four 10″ aluminum pieces and de-burr the ends. Try the shaft in the upper jaw; it should slide freely up and down. Leave the slot in the lower jaw snug enough so that the metal shaft has to be driven in with light hammer blows. Cut out the inside contour of each jaw.

Drill the ⅟₁₆″ hole at the mouth of the long kerf. Jigsaw the kerf through to this hole and smooth the inner face of the kerf with a folded piece of sandpaper.

Draw the lines for the tenon at the front end of the upper jaw. Clamp the jaw in a vise and insert a wedge into the kerf (25). The wedge will permit you to saw off both cheeks of the tenon without scarring the bottom face of the long kerf.

Trace the outline of the lever and jigsaw to shape. Sand the contours smooth and mark off the center mortise. Drill a ¼″ hole through the bottom of the mortise and then remove the mortise with two saw cuts down to the drill hole. Smooth the inner cheeks so that the lever rides snugly around the tenon.

The operating principle of the clamp depends on pressure exerted on the flexible extension under the

25. Kerf wedged for sawing tenon

kerf. This pressure comes from the eccentric motion of the lever, which swings on an off-center axis.

Place the lever on the tenon in the down position and clamp it so it won't move. Drill the off-center hole through lever and tenon. Insert a rivet and peen the end over.

Drive the aluminum shaft into the lower jaw, drill two holes, and rivet. Drill the two holes in the upper jaw that fall on either side of the shaft. Insert the two rivets designed to keep the upper jaw rigid when pressure is applied. A small hole and cotter pin in the upper end of the shaft complete the clamp. Rubber, cork, or felt may be used to line the jaw faces.

Purfling Cutter

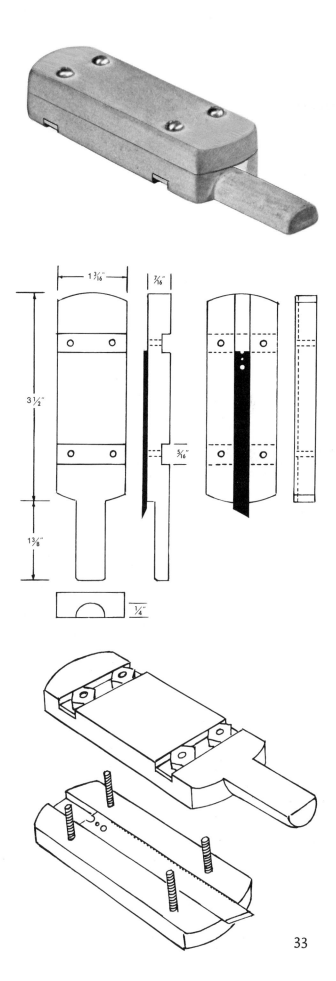

A purfling cutter removes the corner segment around the outer edges of the guitar. The kind of purfling or binding used determines the depth and width of these cut-out ledges. An adjustable purfling cutter designed for the guitar and violin trade is available (20). For those who enjoy making their own tools, an effective cutter can be made from a piece of birch, cherry, or maple and a saber-saw blade.

Slice a $1'' \times 1\frac{3}{16}'' \times 5''$ block open lengthwise and smooth both inner faces. Saw or chisel a groove down the center of side *A*. The groove must be wide enough to accommodate the saber-saw blade and deep enough to hold the blade plus two or three thin metal shims. The depth of the groove must be sized so that the blade and shims will be held firmly in place when the cutter sides are bolted together.

Saw the waste from around the pilot leg of side *B* and shape the pilot to the prescribed shape. Round off the edges of all bearing surfaces to prevent gouging or marking.

A saber-saw blade can be sharpened to a fine cutting edge. The blade pictured is a Trojan S-32. Grind off the teeth along the edge for about $\frac{1}{2}''$ above the cutting edge. In grinding the blade do not allow the blade to overheat and destroy the temper. Sharpen only one edge, the inner face. The shims can be cut from a tin can and flattened. By shifting their position in the grouping, you can achieve a measure of adjustability. If you postpone making the cutter until you have the actual bindings you will use, you can adjust the shimming to work for your arrangement.

Cut two grooves $\frac{5}{16}''$ wide and $\frac{5}{32}''$ deep in the back of side *B*. Cut two strips of metal to act as long washers for the two bolts in each groove. With both sides clamped together, drill four holes and bolt with $\frac{3}{4}''$ machine screws.

33

Round-Bottom Plane

Carving the top and back of an arched-top guitar requires a round-bottom plane. Commercially available round-bottom planes are costly and do not work as well as the plane described here. It is simple, easy to make, and does a good job of quickly removing wood from the large surfaces of an arched-top guitar. Moreover, in active use it will not heat up the way a metal plane will.

The best wood to use for making this plane is cherry (pictured), beech, or maple.

Center the actual size plan on a block of wood $1\frac{3}{16}" \times 1\frac{1}{4}" \times 9"$. Both halves are laid out on the block and after sawing and chiseling are completed, they are cut apart and glued together to form the body of the plane.

Draw the side and top view in position on the block. Make three saw cuts (A, B, C) with a fine backsaw in the side of each half. Cut out the cheek (D) and clean out with chisel and file the tapered slot that holds the wedge. Proper operation of the wedge requires that the slot be uniform on both halves of the plane. Saw apart the halves and glue them together with Titebond or epoxy glue.

Cut the tapered wedge to shape and round the top edges with file and sandpaper. Fit the wedge, making sure the top surface of the wedge makes

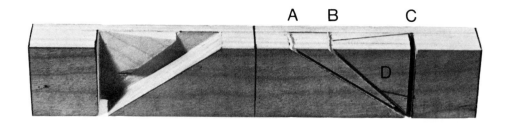

A B C

D

26. Construction sequence for plane

good contact with the slot on both sides. Chisel and file the inner front wall to a concave curve leading down to the bottom exit of the blade.

File and sand the bottom of the plane to its rounded shape. File the opening on the bottom of the plane to a curve that conforms to the curve of the blade cutting edge.

An old saw will provide a piece of metal for a blade. Grind and sharpen the blade to the curve of the cutter exit on the bottom of the plane. The blade should be 2½″ long.

File the edges to their rounded configuration and sand smooth the entire plane.

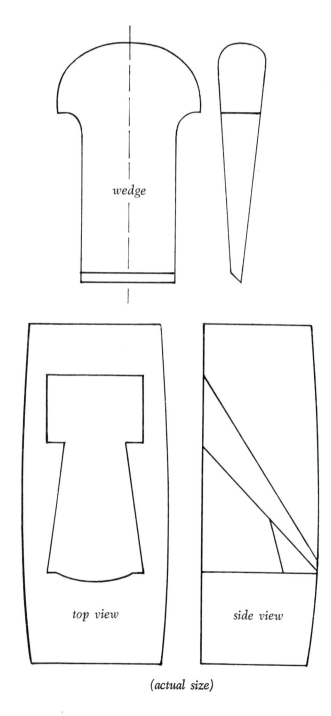

wedge

top view

side view

(actual size)

35

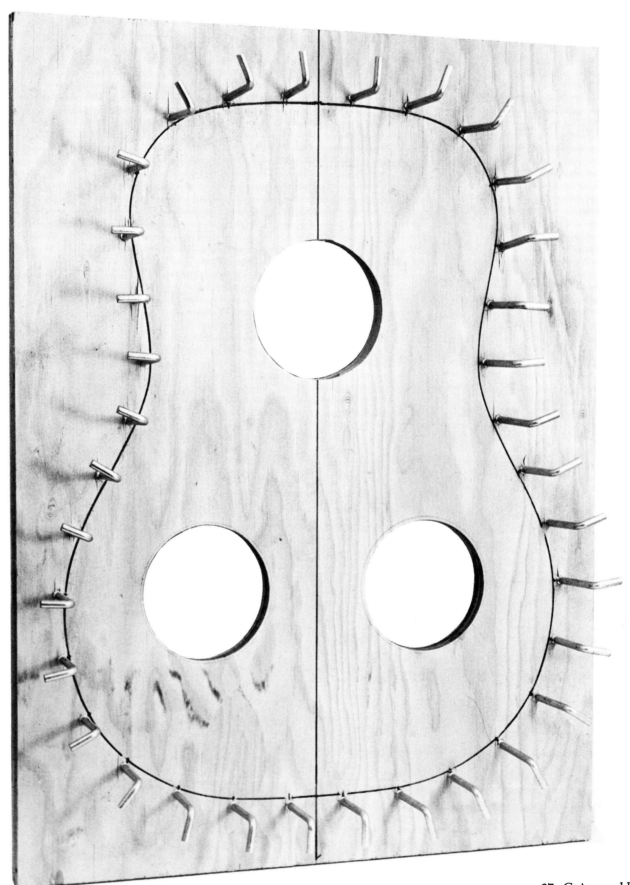

27. Guitar mold

Two simple forms are required to make a steel-string guitar—a mold and a workboard.

The mold is the basic form in which the sound box is assembled and glued together. It is a convenient means of ensuring symmetry during construction and of holding the sides in place while the blocks, linings, and plates (top and back) are glued. Large rubber bands stretched across the box from one L-hook to another apply clamping pressure while the plates are gluing to the sides. The neck is assembled separately and joined to the body when the body is complete.

A workboard is used for making the soundboard and back; the neck of the workboard is clamped to the workbench with the guitar-shaped portion extending clear of the workbench, permitting easy clamping access to all areas of the soundboard and back.

The pattern used here is a slightly modified dreadnought style and can be altered to suit your own preference. Trace both halves of your pattern onto a board to see what the complete shape looks like. When you are satisfied with the shape, trace the half-pattern and transfer the tracing to a stiff sheet of cardboard, Masonite, or thin plywood. Make a template by cutting out the pattern and smoothing the contour. The template is used to transfer the exact shape of the guitar to the top, back, and both sides of the workboard. It is also a useful guide when bending the sides.

Draw a black line down the center of a ¾″ × 18″ × 24″ piece of pressed wood or plywood. Trace the outline of both halves onto the board. At 1″ on either side of the center line at the top, mark off 1⅞″ divisions around the guitar outline with dividers. If you alter the outline, just space these divisions so that they end up about 1″ from either side of the center line at the bottom of the guitar outline. The form shown used seventeen 3″ L-hooks for each half—thirty-four in all. Drill holes for the L-hooks are positioned just outside the outline so that when they are screwed in they just touch the outline.

Cut out the three holes, which (1) lighten the board, (2) permit examination of the sound box interior while the top is gluing to the sides, and (3) pro-

Construction Forms

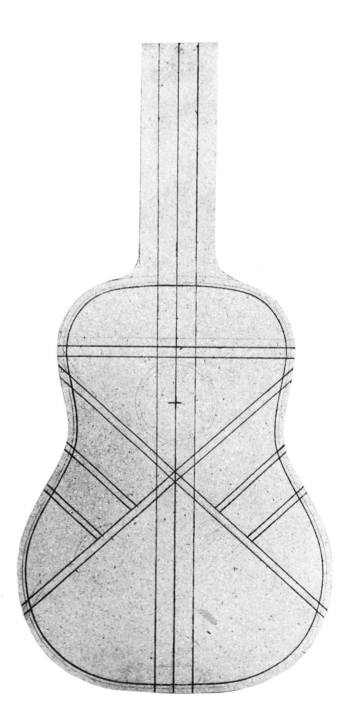

28. Work board

vide handy exits for sweeping out debris that collects. The lower holes were cut with a circle cutter in a drill press. The top hole had to be jigsawed out because of insufficient clearance between the drill press spindle and column.

Drill holes slightly smaller than the L-hook diameter ($\frac{3}{16}$" for the 3" L-hooks) and screw in each hook until no thread is showing. File off any points that may protrude on the other side. This form is now complete.

Cut the workboard out of a $\frac{3}{4}$" $\times$ 18" $\times$ 36" piece of pressed wood or plywood. First draw the center line down the length of the board, with another line 1" away on each side of the center line. Trace in position both halves of the guitar shape with the template. Draw another outline for jigsawing $\frac{1}{2}$" outside the template outline. Repeat this same procedure on both sides of the workboard.

On one side, draw in the strutting and bracing for the soundboard. Use a pointed felt-nib black marker and make sure all elements are carefully drawn in place. Extend all strut and bracing lines past the outline of the guitar to the jigsaw outline. When the top and back are clamped to the workboard, these lines at the edge will indicate the positions of all struts and braces. I have omitted the bottom braces from my workboard because of my penchant for making subtle changes in the bracing of this portion of the soundboard. In any case, being able immediately to spot the correct positions for the major struts and braces is what is important. Jigsaw the workboard to shape, and smooth the rough edges.

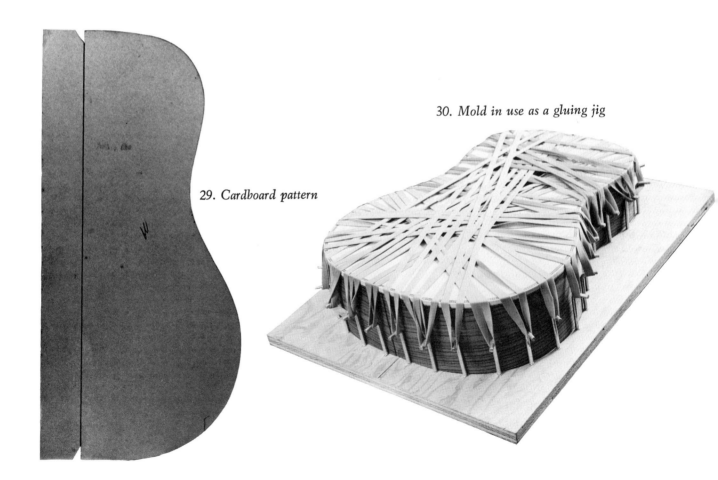

29. Cardboard pattern

30. Mold in use as a gluing jig

31. Trace top half on lower half with tabs fitted
for actual size half pattern

32. *Planing a maple back*

Planing the Wood

Guitar sides and back are sold in matched sets by suppliers (see list of suppliers in appendix) and are at least ⅛" thick. The wood is often still rough from sawing.

Clamp the end of a side near the edge of the workbench. Remove the high spots with a plane adjusted to remove a small amount of wood at a time. Move the plane away from you with the plane at a slight angle to cut with a shearing action. Lift the plane, return to the beginning, and make another cut. If the plane bucks, you are cutting against the grain and will have to plane from the opposite direction. Plane the surface of each side until all rough saw marks are gone.

With both sides level, switch to the hand scraper. I use a Red Devil #50 2½"-wide hand scraper. It is sold with replacement blades, and a few passes with a fine, flat file will set a good cutting edge. Round the corners of each cutting edge so they won't gouge the wood. Properly sharpened, the scraper will remove wood just as fast as a cabinet scraper blade. Apart from the ease of keeping the Red Devil blade sharp, it is much less tiring to use than a cabinet scraper blade because both hands can be used to apply pressure (33) instead of just the thumbs. Draw the scraper toward you, its blade angled for shear, moving in a systematic pattern to ensure even removal of wood. Check the thickness frequently as work proceeds. Switch to a large cabinet scraper blade for final smoothing and leveling. Sanding is unnecessary.

Clamp the two sides butted edge to edge and use the scraper blade over both. Turn them over, butt the other edges, and repeat the same procedure. When finished they should be a uniform ⅝₄".

The back is not planed to thickness until after the two halves are jointed. Fasten the jointed back to the board used for the jointing operation. Drive some tacks in along the perimeter to immobilize the back while planing and scraping. Drive the tacks in next to the edge, not into the back itself.

Plane and scrape both surfaces using the same procedure as for the sides. Because of the large area of the back, it is necessary to check the level of the surface with a straightedge. Smooth the back to a uniform thickness of ³⁄₃₂".

Smooth both sides of the jointed spruce top, removing only as much wood as necessary to make both sides smooth. Smoothing will permit you to judge which side is best for the top face and will leave the maximum thickness for inlaying whatever you plan for the sound hole decoration. Top thickness should be no less than ⅞₄".

A persistent misconception is the belief that a soundboard should be thicker on the bass side. Frank Hubbard, in his fine book *Three Centuries of Harpsichord Making* (Harvard University Press, 1965), points out that "analogy was too strong for the old makers"; bass strings and sounds were heavier so they made the soundboard thicker on the bass side. Some modern piano makers taper their soundboards in the reverse direction. A thin soundboard is in fact resonant to a lower frequency than a thick one because the thick board is stiffer. But the nature of bass and treble sound frequencies may also be a factor. Bass frequencies have an amorphous omnidirectional character, while treble frequencies travel in a direct line from the point of emission.

I always plane the top to a uniform thickness and taper the perimeter slightly just before installing the purfling.

Store the top and back under a weighted board until they are strutted and braced. If an appreciable amount of time is going to elapse before you resume work—two or three weeks—shellac the end grain of top and back to retard the absorption of moisture.

33. Scraping side with hand scraper

34. Final leveling with cabinet scraper blade

Neck

Steel-string guitar necks, especially those with fourteen frets clear of the body, are under extraordinary strain. String pressure at standard pitch (A440) ranges from 160 to well over 200 lbs depending on string gauge and scale. Necks must be built to withstand this constant strain, and numerous methods for reinforcing these slender extensions have been devised.

Necks designed for use with compound and light gauge strings can be reinforced with a variety of steel rods: T-bar, channel bar, square tubing, or narrow bar stock. Ebony strips of ¼" × ½" have also been used with success. Regardless of which is used, these factors must be taken into account: if you can bend the rod or bar with hand pressure it will not work; if the exposed metal surface has a width of more than ⅜" it should be buried with a thin strip of covering wood; if the reinforcement weighs more than 4 or 5 oz the neck is going to be heavy, an important consideration whether you play for long periods with the guitar in your lap or supported by a neck sling. The added neck weight will, however, increase the loudness of the guitar by damping neck oscillation. This movement of the neck tends to dissipate the amplitude of sound box resonance.

Adjustable tension or truss rods are used in guitars with heavier-gauge strings. Numerous methods exist for "loading" these devices, but their operating principle is the same; tightening an adjustable nut exerts upward pressure on that central portion of the

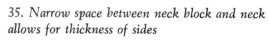

35. *Narrow space between neck block and neck allows for thickness of sides*

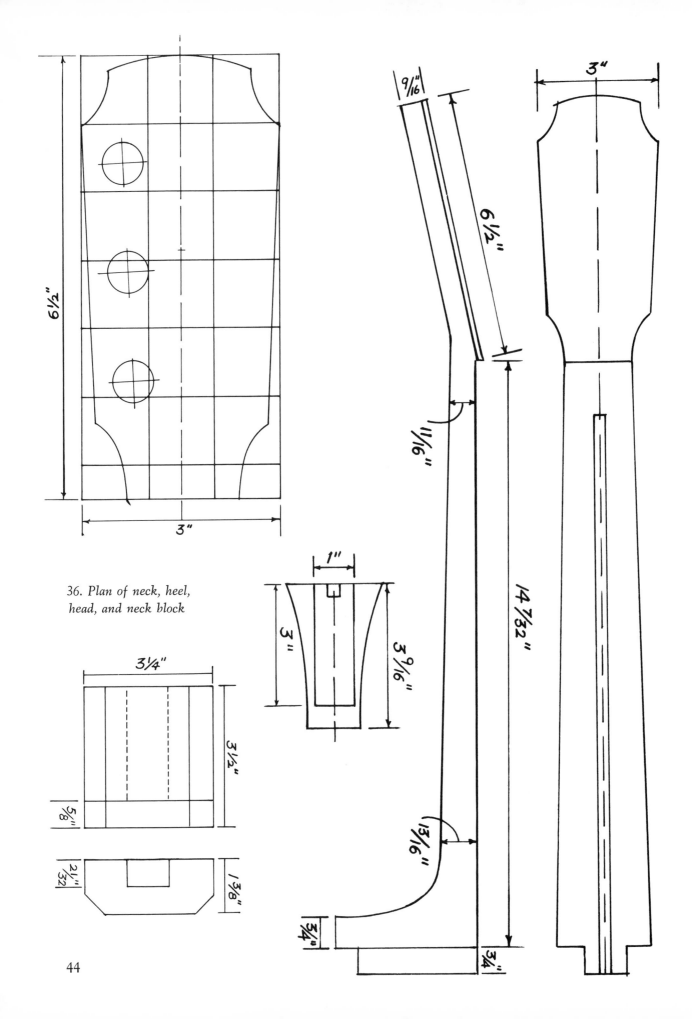

36. *Plan of neck, heel,
head, and neck block*

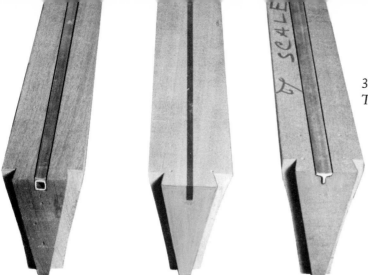

37. *Square tube, ebony strip, and T-bar reinforcement*

neck most likely to bow. Truss rods are designed to remedy concave bowing of the neck. They cannot cure a twisted neck or one with back bow.

In my guitar I use a strip of ¼" × ½" 2024 T3 aluminum bar stock (not to be confused with the soft aluminum sold in hardware stores). 2024 T3 is a heat-hardened, tempered grade of aluminum used in the airplane industry and has a yield point of 44,000 psi. It is very strong and rigid and has one third the weight of a comparable bar in steel. The center bar and two end pieces total 2½" oz. In order for the neck to bow, the center bar would have to bow, and the end stops reinforce the ability of the center bar to resist bowing. All the pieces are let into the neck carefully butted to ensure maximum strength.

A dovetailed joint (152) is the standard method used for joining neck to body. In factory procedure this is quickly and accurately accomplished with a jigged shaper setup. A dovetailed joint is a strong, efficient joint with several advantages: Its wedge-shaped tenon gives it a locking action that holds the heel of the neck tightly against the body, and the long tapered shape of the tenon makes the neck easy to remove for repair or resetting. A drawback for the novice builder is that it requires considerable skill with a chisel to cut an accurate dovetailed tenon and mortise by hand.

I use a straight mortise-and-tenon joint that can easily be cut with a saw and is locked in position with two dowels when the neck is aligned. It is just as strong a joint and is designed to pull the heel in

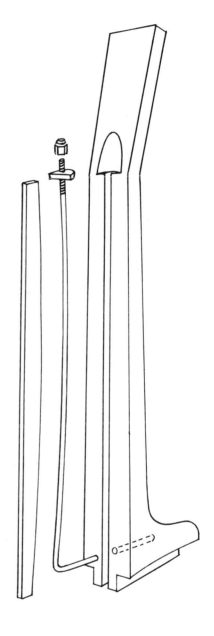

38. *Adjustable truss rod made of ³⁄₁₆" drill rod bent over on lower end and inserted into hole drilled into heel. Pre-curved rod is set into curved channel with curved wood inset glued in place over it. Tightening the adjusting nut applies upward pressure on central portion of neck. (D'Aquisto design)*

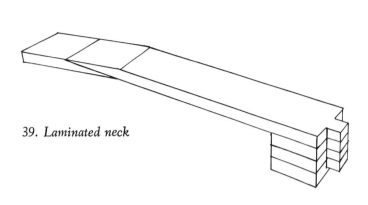

39. Laminated neck

40. Clamping head piece to neck

tight against the body when the neck is finally glued in place. The mortised block that receives the neck tenon is prepared when the neck is made and glued into the body later.

The neck can be band sawed out of a block of mahogany or laminated of several pieces (39). Use wood sawn on the quarter with end grain running at right angles to the top of the neck. If the end grain is slanted more than 45°, the board should be sawn in half lengthwise, one half flipped end over end, and reglued. If you have this situation, you can glue in a center strip of ebony that will give you a black line down the underside of the neck.

If you wish to adapt the basic plan to a different fret scale or fingerboard width, begin by making a cardboard model of your fingerboard. Mark the four-

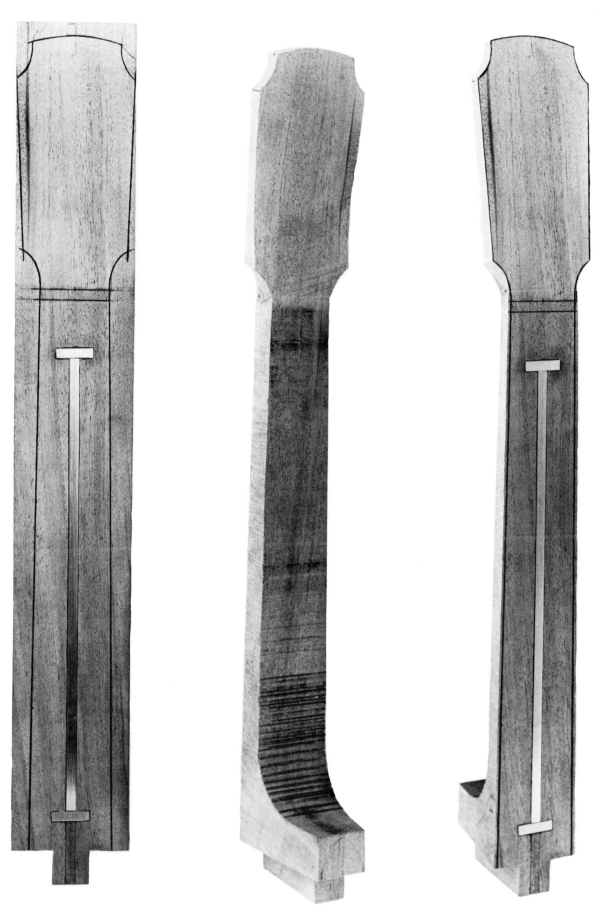

41. Neck at various stages of construction sequence

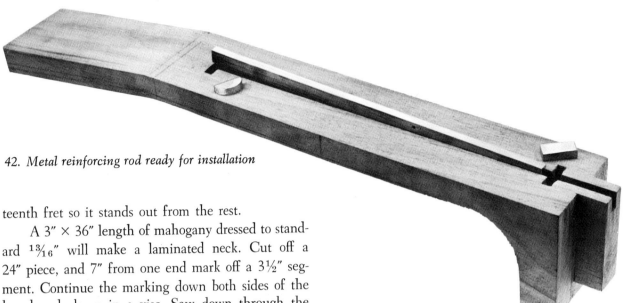

42. *Metal reinforcing rod ready for installation*

teenth fret so it stands out from the rest.

A 3″ × 36″ length of mahogany dressed to standard $^{13}/_{16}$″ will make a laminated neck. Cut off a 24″ piece, and 7″ from one end mark off a 3½″ segment. Continue the marking down both sides of the board and clamp in a vise. Saw down through the board on the angle formed by the line bisecting the 3½″ rectangle. Reverse the cut-off small piece and place it on top of the longer piece so that the oblique cut makes a continuous line.

Clamp the two pieces on the edge of the workbench and plane their angled face smooth and square. Check with a try square to make sure the angled surface is level and square with the edges of the boards.

Reverse their positions and glue the head portion to the neck (40). Apply Titebond to each face and clamp each piece to the workbench with a vertical clamp. Keep these clamps loose until the glued faces are in contact. Tighten the vertical clamps and apply the horizontal clamps using cauls. The vertical clamps are used to prevent movement of the glued joint under the pressure of the horizontal clamps. A piece of waxed paper under the joint will keep it from being glued to the workbench.

When dry, clamp again to the edge of the workbench so that the inclined head protrudes out from the bench. Plane the face of the head smooth and level.

The head of the guitar is where luthiers have traditionally applied their personal hallmark; the profile of the head identifies the maker. A well-balanced design requires thoughtful consideration and preliminary sketch work.

The head is customarily faced with rosewood veneer or a sandwich of rosewood over holly or maple veneer that will expose a decorative white line in the finished head. Ebony veneer can also be used for facing the head but will probably contain light streaks that will require staining to get a jet black surface. In my design I use an underlay of ⅛″ rosewood faced with a thin veneer of Thuya burl and edged with ebony. Fitting the ebony edge is a demanding task requiring skilled use of fretsaw and scraper blade, a good test of woodworking skill. No matter what facing scheme you use, the final thickness of the head should be $^9/_{16}$″.

Glue the face veneer—or sandwich—to the head, leaving a small overhang that will later be sawn off to backstop the nut. Cut the pieces for the heel lamination and glue them together with Titebond. When dry, glue this assembly to the bottom of the neck.

Carefully pencil a line down the center of the top of the neck, continuing down the vertical front face of the vertical end. Mark off the tenon and saw out the blocks on both sides of the tenon. Draw the shape of the fretboard on the top face of the neck.

Plow a ¼″ groove down the center of the neck with bench saw or chisel. Finish off the upper terminus with a chisel if you plow the groove with a bench saw. The groove should slope up toward the head so that the reinforcing bar will be ½″ at the bottom and $^7/_{16}$″ at the top. File off protruding metal.

Chisel out the mortises for the end stops. Glue in all the pieces with Titebond and fill the remaining slot at the bottom with a mahogany inset. An important point in fitting the reinforcing bar is that it should go in snug without any force that might split the neck.

Cut out the mortised block, making sure the mortise is sized to a snug fit with the tenon. Glue on the bottom piece of the block. Cut off the bottom of the tenon so it rests in the mortise with the bottom of the block and heel flush. The space left between the top of the block and the top of the tenon will be taken up by the thickness of the soundboard.

Trace your design onto the face of the head and jigsaw it out leaving some tolerance for final smoothing of the contours.

Cut a cardboard template of the heel contour and trace the shape in position on each side of the tenon. Holding a saw so that its angle undercuts the neck, saw from the heel all the way down to the neck. Leave 1/16" clearance on each side of the fretboard. Saw out both sides in the same manner.

Clamp the neck to the edge of the workbench (46) using the edge of the face veneer as a backstop and with a block of wood clamped alongside the neck.

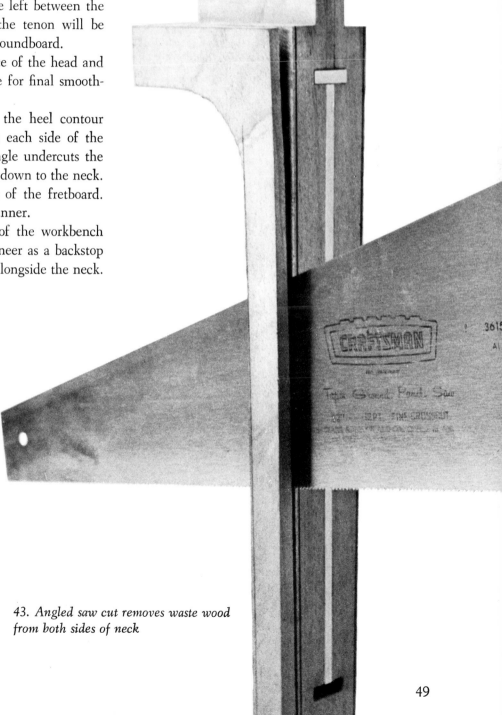

43. *Angled saw cut removes waste wood from both sides of neck*

49

This will prevent movement of the neck while each side in turn is shaped with the spokeshave. Work slowly and carefully, checking frequently to make sure that the shape conforms to the blueprint. Use a chisel to carve the rounded terminus of the neck under the head.

Shape the heel to its final form using gouge and rasp. I also use a four-in-one shoe rasp for shaping the neck and heel. Cut away the largest chunks of waste wood with a 1″ gouge struck by hammer or mallet. Properly sharpened, it will cut with hand pressure alone. Place both your feet squarely and use the weight and leverage of your entire torso to work the tool. Don't try to take out too much wood with one cut. Guide the blade with a firm grip of your left hand and apply pressure with the handle held securely under the heel of your right palm.

As the long curve of the heel where it butts against the body takes shape, beware of dislodging large splinters with the chisel—easy to do when the edge of the gouge is cutting parallel to the grain. Work to within a small distance of the edge of the contour and finish with sandpaper.

A good precaution is to fasten a piece of cardboard or scrap veneer to the front face of the head with rubber bands or tape.

Carefully smooth the neck to its final shape, but keep slightly outside the lines marking the position of the fretboard.

Drill the holes in the head for the tuning machines. The machine bushings should go in with some gentle forcing. Clamp the head facedown to a protective piece of wood when drilling the holes to avoid splintering the face veneer.

44. Carving heel with 1″ gouge

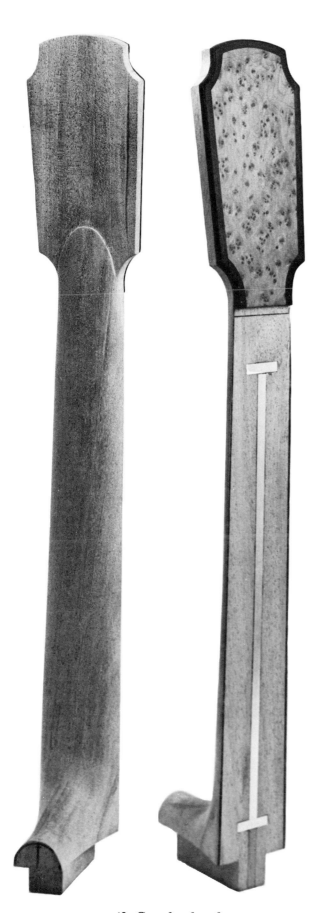

48. Completed neck

45. Rounding neck with spokeshave

46. Roughing out shape with rasp

47. Chiseling neck finial to shape

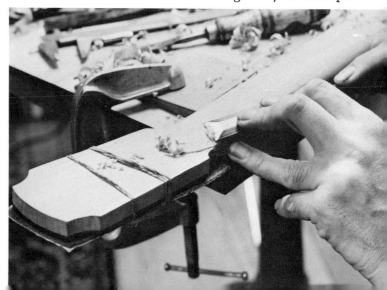

Front disc detail

49. Bending iron with propane torch

Bending the Sides

A heated pipe is the traditional tool for bending guitar sides, and a perfectly satisfactory bending iron can be made for a modest sum. The following parts are needed:

A 12″ length of copper, brass, or aluminum pipe (not iron) at least 3″ in diameter

Two pieces of ⁵⁄₁₆″ × 13″ threaded steel rod

A 5½″ × 6″ square of asbestos

Eight ⁵⁄₁₆″ nuts and washers

A 2″ × 6″ × 12″ board

Two 1″ × 3½″ × 5″ blocks of wood

A metal disc slightly larger than the pipe diameter

Fasten a disc to the front end of the pipe to seal it off and contain the heat. Cut the disc to the inside diameter of the pipe leaving three tabs protruding to fit into corresponding cutouts in the pipe. The tabs

protrude slightly beyond the slots and are hammered over to lock them in place. In my pipe I also have a disc set into the back end so the walls of the pipe won't buckle. A large hole in the center of this disc accommodates the burner tip. If the walls of your pipe are thick enough you will not need this back disc. A propane torch supported by a cradle stand provides heat.

A steel-string guitar, with its rather shallow waist curve, requires a large-diameter pipe for efficient bending. For a guitar with a sharply incurved waist, the pipe diameter cannot exceed the radius of this curve. An arched-top guitar with a cutaway section requires a small-diameter pipe to bend that section. Always use the largest diameter pipe that will still do the job.

Bend the threaded rods into U-shaped bolts that fit the pipe. Drill four ⁵⁄₁₆″ holes through the asbestos and board and fasten the completed pipe with the U-bolts. Use nuts and washers both above and below; the bottom nuts pull the U-bolts tight against the pipe and the top nuts are then screwed down tight. Glue the wood blocks on each end of the board to keep the bolt ends clear of the workbench. Make the cradle stand the right height for the burner tip to fit into the pipe.

Cut a template of cardboard to 3½″ × 30½″ × 4⁵⁄₁₆″. The standard wedge or taper of a dreadnought guitar is 3¾″ at the heel, 4¾″ at the bottom. I have lowered the sides to achieve a better balance between treble and bass with some small sacrifice of bass resonance and loudness. Decreasing the volume of air in the sound box raises its resonating pitch, a principle easily observed by blowing across the mouth of a small bottle and then a jug.

Changing the side height to affect volume is entirely a personal matter based on player preference. The 4¾″ bottom, however, is about the outer limit for a flat-top acoustic. Above this size the guitar will start sounding boom-y rather than just bass-y.

Trace the shape of your template onto the sides making sure that the taper is properly oriented on each side. Center the template so there is some overlap on each end. Cut out each side, but do not cut off the ends.

Some guitar makers prefer to soak the wood for several hours or even overnight before bending. Others find that just moistening the wood occasionally with a sponge during bending is sufficient.

Bending wood is simple if you follow these rules. Work slowly, applying steady pressure without sudden or abrupt changes in pressure. Before the wood will actually start to bend, it must be heated over a larger portion than the main contact area. This is accomplished by slowly rocking the board while steadily maintaining pressure. As the wood gets hotter, pressure is increased bit by bit until bending occurs.

As bending proceeds, use the template to check the curve. Be sure you are placing the bends in the correct surface so that you don't wind up with two pieces for one side.

If a surface fracture opens up during bending— a common occurrence with curly maple—don't be alarmed; it can probably be glued down tight. If you still have a long way to go with the bending of the fractured portion, use a piece of canvas or sheet metal to hold the fracture down during bending. After bending is completed, glue the fracture closed.

Place the bent sides in the mold to make sure they conform to the mold.

50. Rock wood with steadily increasing, gentle pressure

Side Assembly

Fit the bent sides into the mold. A perfect fit is not important, but symmetry is. Press the sides against the L-hooks and fashion a small wooden prop, slightly incurved at the ends, to prop the sides at the waist. Align both sides and clamp their overlap at each end. Using a try square, draw a vertical line down the center of the ends exactly coincident with the center line drawn on the mold.

Carefully saw down through the overlap and smooth the edges so they can be edge-glued. Apply Titebond and use adhesive tape to keep the edges in contact while they are gluing. When dry, clean and smooth the inner surface of the bottom joint and the lower part of the top joint.

Glue the top block in place with Titebond, making sure that the center line of the block is aligned with the center line of the mold. Do not center the block on the edge-glued joint because that may be slightly off. It doesn't matter if it is off, but the block must be on dead center.

The tail block may have to be glued up out of two pieces of mahogany to get the block to the correct height with the grain horizontal. Saw and smooth the block to shape, and round the back to conform exactly to the slight curve of the bottom where it will be glued. This is important so that the block will hold the curve and not distort it when clamped.

Glue and clamp the tail block (52) using waxed paper between wood and cauls. The outside caul is a block of ¼" plywood that easily bends to distribute the clamping pressure more evenly over the curved surface.

After the blocks are glued, the sides must be carefully checked to make sure that both sides are of equal height along their entire length. With the top edge of the sides facedown in the mold, measure the sides at different places and eliminate any unevenness. Lay the workboard on top of the side assembly, a simple way of checking the level of each side. Invert the side assembly and repeat the procedure. Both sides must be of equal height and touch the floor of the mold at all points before lining can be installed.

Preparing an inlay strip to cover the bottom

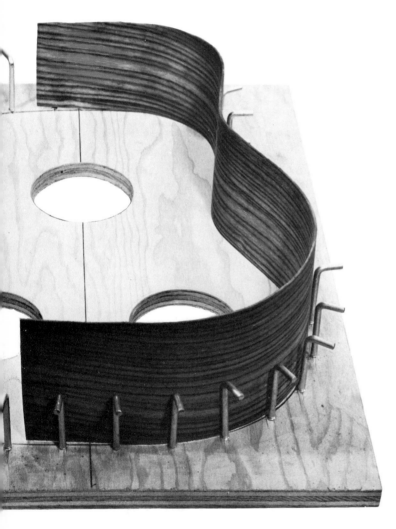

51. Side fitted in mold

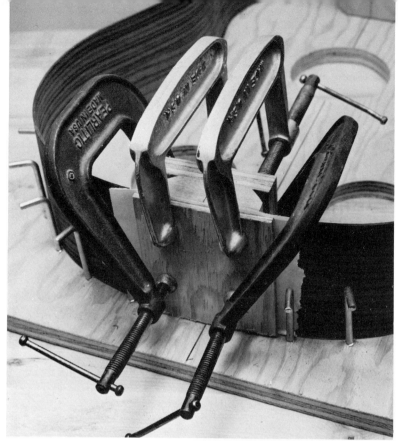

52. *Clamping tail block to sides*

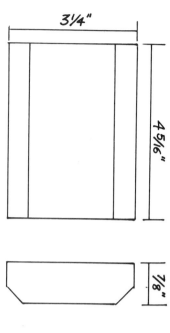

53. *Plan of tail block*

54. *Checking bottom inlay for snug fit*

center joint is the final step in making the sides. Glue up a ⅜" × 5" strip of veneer or plastic (depending on the purfling you will use) with a strip of black-white purfling along each long edge. Do this on waxed paper, using push pins or brads to press the veneer strips against the center strip during gluing.

Transfer the width of the completed inlay to the bottom joint. If the center joint is not in alignment with the center line of the mold, make sure that the inlay is. Clamp the side in a vise with the joint facing up. Using a try square as a sawing guide, saw to the depth of the inlay with a fine backsaw. Chisel out the groove and level with a file. Set the inlay aside because it is not glued in place until the edge purfling is completed.

If you plan an end pin for your guitar, glue a 1" strip of ¹⁄₁₆" maple or other hardwood down the center of the inner face of the tail block. This is a precautionary measure against the tail block's splitting, and the grain of the strip must run vertically. The end pin hole is drilled and reamed to fit just before the finish is applied.

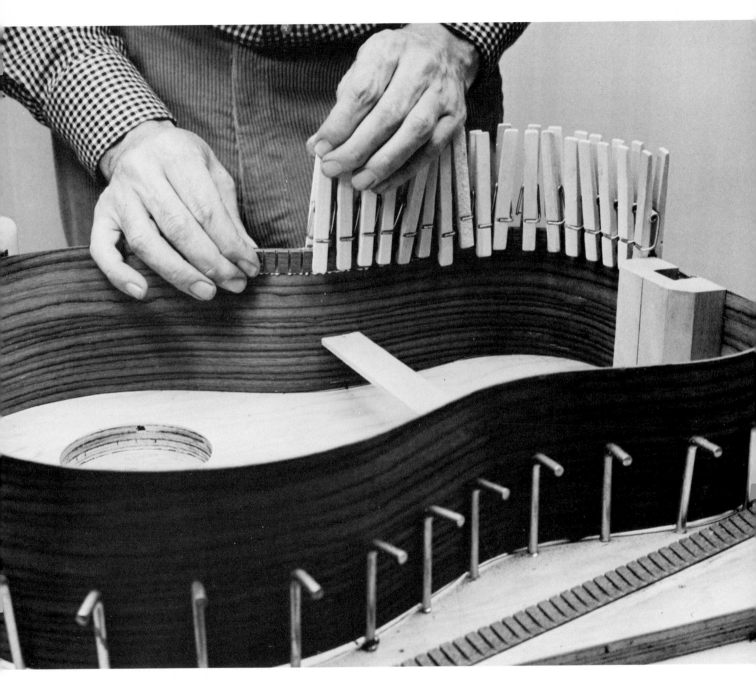

55. *Installing kerfed lining (note prop in place)*

Linings

Linings provide a broader gluing surface for the plates and strengthen the sides. They are continuous strips kerfed (partly sawed through) at ¼″ intervals. Basswood and mahogany are commonly used for lining. Allow for four strips of 30″, and they need not be continuous—10″ or 12″ strips are fine and easier to handle. No acoustic benefit derives from gluing in a kerfed lining in one piece.

Lining is obtainable from suppliers, cut to the proper triangular shape. Kerfing can be done quickly with a radial saw, but if you don't have one you can kerf lining in a small miter box. Clamp a block of wood to the saw blade so that the saw stops ⅟₃₂″ from the floor of the box. Save time and effort by spot gluing two linings together. Apply a dab of white glue every 7″ or 8″ and kerf them both at the same time.

Keep the connecting spine between blocks no thicker than ⅟₃₂″ because the lining will not clamp tight to the sides unless the lining is flexible enough to conform easily to the curve of the sides.

Always install lining with the sides in the mold, prop in place. Apply Titebond to a section and fit the segment tight against the top block. Clamp with clothespins and fit each segment so that the final appearance looks like an unbroken continuous strip. If a section fractures while gluing, saw off the fragmented end to the next clean juncture and glue in place. Inspect the lining top and bottom for glue drips and clean away all squeeze-out with a small dampened brush or cloth. After all the linings are in, check their bottom seams for gaps. Fill all gaps with Titebond.

Mystic (self-adhering) cloth tape is sold in various colors and in 1″ and 1½″ widths. Apply five strips of 1½″ brown tape equally spaced around each side as reinforcement. If you use 1″ tape, use eight strips on each side. Paste them in place after the top lining is in. Use a small piece of lining to mark off the other end for cutting before installing the bottom lining. Fit each end up to the lining and not under it. Smooth the tapes down so that they are stuck tight to the wood. Cloth reinforcement for thin sides is an ancient practice and was used by Stradivarius to reinforce the sides of his cellos. Its main purpose in guitars is to prevent cracking of the sides.

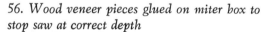

56. Wood veneer pieces glued on miter box to stop saw at correct depth

57. *Cutting off cloth tape reinforcement*

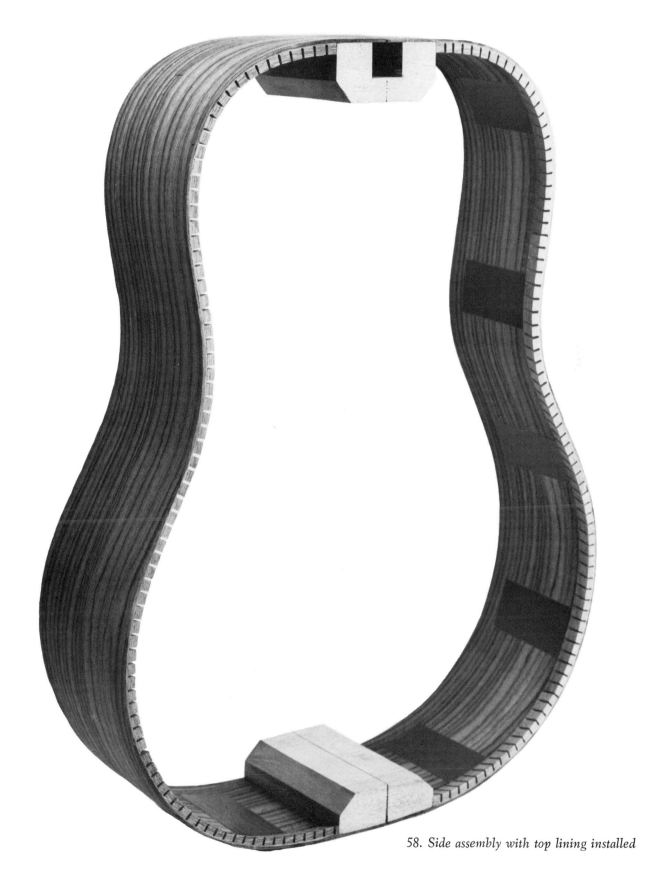

58. *Side assembly with top lining installed*

Jointing Top and Back

The halves of the soundboard are joined along the edge where the grain is narrowest. Close the two halves like a book and match the grain on the end so that the halves are placed exactly as they were before being cut apart.

Clamp the boards in a vise and plane the edges to be joined as level as possible. Do not remove any more wood than necessary to accomplish this end.

A 2′ length of 1″ × 3″ lumber that is perfectly true in its long dimension will complete the jointing of the edges. Cut a sheet of medium-grit (#80-D) aluminum oxide paper into strips wide enough to glue along the 1″ edge of the 1″ × 3″ board. Glue the strips in place edge to edge so they make a long, unbroken sanding surface. An aluminum level (59) works very well. Sandpaper can be glued with rubber cement or double-faced tape.

Place one half of the soundboard on top of the other, overlapping so that only one edge is brought into contact with the sandpaper. Hold the boards down firmly with your left hand and slide the sanding edge back and forth against the edge of the board. Continue this sanding until the edge looks true. Reverse the boards and sand the other edge. Butt the two edges together and hold them up before a light. If light can be seen through the joint, repeat the sanding until no light is visible through the joint.

With the jointed boards butted, trace the outline of your guitar template on each half. Position the template so that the best half of the soundboard becomes the bottom or main vibrating surface. Blemishes and grain irregularities can sometimes be concealed under the fretboard.

Lay the halves down on a ¾″ plywood board at least 20″ × 20″. Press the joint together and examine it closely. Sometimes the darker lines in the grain will meet in a disturbing pattern at the joint if the grain converges. Occasionally an unsightly heavy line will result from the merging of two dark lines. For the most unobtrusive joint, sand the edges until they give the appearance of an unbroken grain pattern

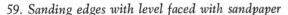

59. Sanding edges with level faced with sandpaper

when butted.

Center the soundboard on the plywood work-board. Drive five carpet tacks along the outer edge of one side so that their heads grip the board and hold it firm. Put a strip of waxed paper under the jointed edge and position a ¼″ × ¾″ batten centered under this edge. Position the other half of the sound-board so the two gluing edges are in contact over the batten. Drive in five tacks along the outer edge of this half, but not far enough to engage the wood.

Remove this half of the soundboard and apply a thin coat of clear epoxy cement to the gluing edge. Remove the batten and coat the other half's edge with epoxy. Replace the batten, put the loose half back into position, and hammer the tacks down so they grip the edge. Place a strip of waxed paper over the joint and pull out the batten. Clamp a long board over the glued joint. For uniform pressure the clamping board should be slightly bowed. The board serves only to hold the two edges aligned during gluing and should not be so tightly clamped at the ends that the middle of the board rises. Leave un-disturbed overnight.

Do not unclamp the soundboard until you first remove the tacks from one edge. If the clamping board is released before the tacks are lifted, the joint may fly up and rupture, leaving you with the annoy-ing task of resanding the edges and gluing the halves together again.

The basic procedure for gluing the back is identical with that described for the soundboard. The only difference is the use of a center strip of inlay on the back, a traditional embellishment. A light strip is used with rosewood and a dark strip with maple or other light wood.

Veneer strips are trimmed to the thickness of the back and sandwiched between the butted edges over the batten. All edges are coated with epoxy and clamped as before.

Inlay or marquetry strips that are the standard veneer thickness (1⁄28″) cannot be sandwiched. The halves must be glued and a channel routed over the joint to the width of the inlay.

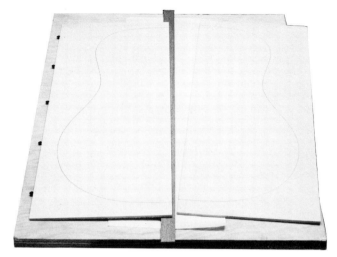

60. *One edge tacked, batten in position*

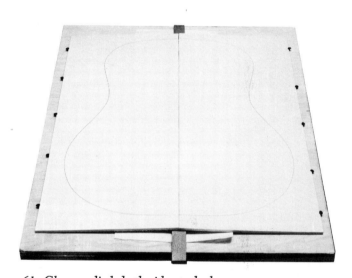

61. *Glue applied, both sides tacked*

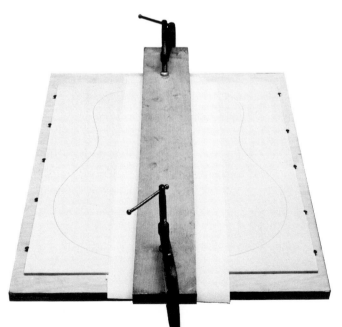

62. *Batten removed, joint under pressure*

Soundboard and Back

Antonio de Torres Jurado, a key figure in the development of the modern guitar (1817–1892), was the author of a famous experiment. He built a guitar with a spruce soundboard and a papier-mâché body to demonstrate the fundamental importance of a fan-braced soundboard in the production of tone. The instrument reportedly had a fine tone.

It is probable that Torres proved not only the primacy of the soundboard in tone production but also the importance of a body that is flexible. And we know from an examination of the instruments of Torres and the great makers who followed him that all bracing and thicknessing of guitars were designed for the strategic employment of this flexing.

Imagine a guitar made of rubber. If you struck the top, the back and sides would bulge, rebound, and repeat this motion in subsiding degree until at rest. If an iron frame were inserted, making the peripheral boundaries rigid, a blow would produce a different result. The top would vibrate, but only briefly because the back and sides could not assist in prolonging this vibration.

A sense of this horizontal, vertical, and torsional flexing must remain central in the builder's considerations while he is constructing a guitar. And the challenge is not to make the guitar as flexible as possible, but to control and utilize flexing to produce superior tone.

The slight arching of the back has been a consistent feature of the finest guitars. An obvious reason is that arching prevents the illusion of concavity often observed in perfectly flat, dark surfaces. A more compelling reason is that arching improves the tone of a guitar.

Going back to our flexible rubber guitar, a blow on the top will move top, back, and sides. But because movement is unhampered by internal bracing, the back and sides are free not only to bulge but also to bounce back inward beyond the normal plane of these surfaces while at rest. Arching the back is clearly intended to limit and define its vibratory motion. Bracing the soundboard performs the same function of controlling its movement as well as adding strength.

Arching and bracing serve the purpose of disciplining the movement of the principal vibrating surfaces in a manner designed to enhance tone. In the same way, adding or subtracting from the thickness of both plates and sides must be done in a degree that assists the overall character of this controlled flexing.

Each time the luthier builds an instrument, he pits his experience, skill, and intuition against the possibilities hidden in a few pieces of wood. Building a guitar is fairly easy. Building a really good one is hard.

Soundboard Construction

Smooth the top to an overall thickness of $\frac{7}{64}''$. Place the template in position on the soundboard and trace the guitar shape. Locate the sound hole center and lightly mark off the sound hole cutout and the inner and outer edges of the grooves that will be cut to receive the veneer inlay strips or rosette. If you plan to use the simple veneer strip trim (commercial guitar style), be sure to plan on one encircling strip about $\frac{1}{8}''$ from the hole's edge. This is necessary to strengthen the end-grain wood that runs into the sound hole and to prevent cracks.

A drill press and circle cutter are the fastest system for cutting sound hole grooves and the hole itself. Set the cutter depth for the thickness of your inlay, but not to exceed $\frac{3}{64}''$. There is no reason to weaken the soundboard unnecessarily by applying a deep inlay. Standard veneer thickness ($\frac{1}{28}''$) is plenty.

Work shy of your markings when setting the cutter because centrifugal force will enlarge the

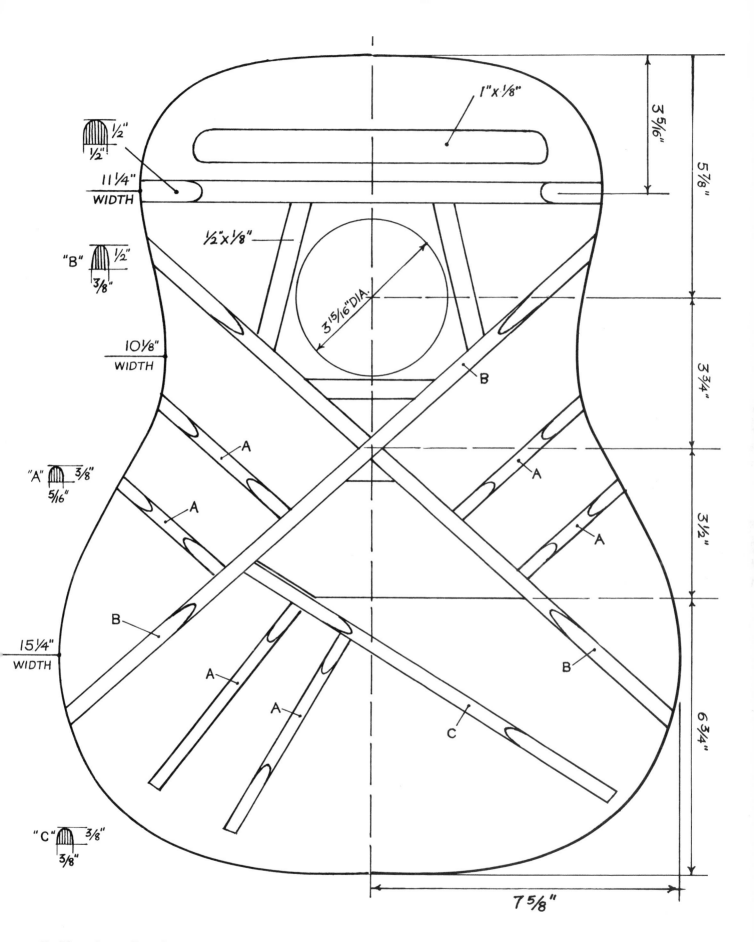

1" x ⅛"

½"
½"

11¼"
WIDTH

½" x ⅛"

3 5/16"

5⅞"

3 15/16" DIA.

"B"
½"
⅜"

B

3¾"

10⅛"
WIDTH

A

A

A

"A"
⅜"
5/16"

A

A

3½"

B

B

15¼"
WIDTH

A

A

C

6¾"

"C"
⅜"
⅜"

7⅝"

63. Plan of soundboard

cutting radius when the blade is working far from the center drill. Cut the inner and outer edges and clean out wide grooves by moving the cutter a bit at a time.

If you don't have a drill press, a compass fitted with a cutter blade is the cheapest and simplest way of making veneer strip grooves. Drill a $\frac{1}{16}$" hole in the center of a piece of metal at least $\frac{1}{16}$" $\times$ 2" $\times$ 2". Position the hole exactly over the center of the sound hole and glue with Scotch Super Strength adhesive. Keep the glue away from the hole so that the latter doesn't fill.

Buy a blister card of Grifhold #24-E stencil cutter knives sold in hobby or art supply shops. These blades will fit in the leg of most compasses. The compass shown is a Vemco #S570; it is inexpensive and has a wheel adjustment, which is essential for accuracy. Reverse the metal point in the other leg so that the flat, cut-off end is in working position. This end goes into the small hole in the metal plate

and will give you a solid, nonshifting axis.

Make sure the blade is razor sharp, and cut the outlines with several passes on each incision. Do not try to cut to the proper depth with just one pass. Reverse the blade when cutting inner edges so that the knife bevel always faces into the groove and the outer walls remain vertical.

After incising the edges, cut a bevel down to each edge with a sharp knife. Clean away the rest of the waste wood in the grooves with a small chisel. This can also be quickly accomplished with a router and small bit.

If your veneer strips are glued up in a ring you may have to slice open the ring to fit them into their grooves. Position the sliced opening where the fretboard will lie. Brush white glue into the grooves and press home the strips. If the grooves are properly sized, the strips should require a bit of gentle forcing to seat them. Use waxed paper, a board, and weights —several bricks perhaps—to apply pressure until dry.

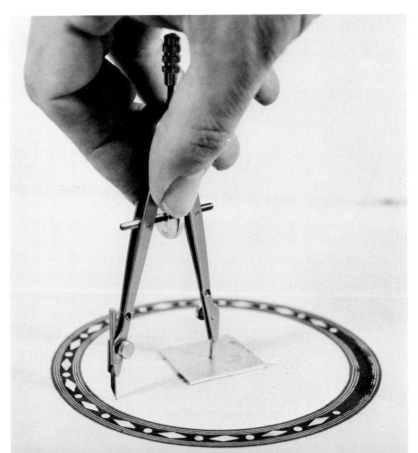

64. Non-shifting axis for compass cutter

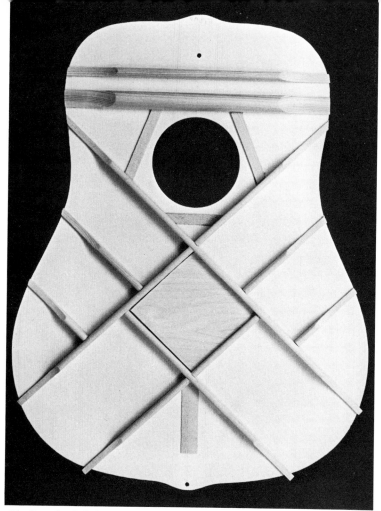

65. *Standard Gibson six-string flat-top bracing*

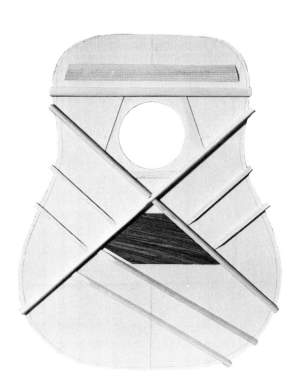

66. *Martin D-18, D-28, D-35 bracing*

67. *Martin twelve-string bracing*

If you are inlaying a mosaic rosette and have to cut out a piece to make it fit, make this cut at the least attractive point in the rosette. Position the cut portion and other flaws in the area that will be concealed by the fretboard.

Coat the groove with white glue and press the rosette into place. Tap the rosette home with a mallet over a wooden caul to receive the blows. Quickly, while the glue is still wet, raise some fine spruce sawdust by sanding near the rosette. Press this sawdust into any gaps around the edge of the rosette. Use waxed paper and a weighted board to apply pressure.

When dry, cut out the sound hole itself and trim all protruding veneers flush with the face of the soundboard. Complete the leveling process with a single-edge razor blade used as a scraper. Sandpaper will wear away the softer spruce much faster than the hardwood mosaic and will also grind darker woods of the mosaic into the lighter woods. A razor blade will produce a clean, smooth finish.

With the inlay completed, jigsaw the outline of the soundboard. Lay the soundboard facedown in the mold and position the side assembly on top of it. Make sure the top and sides are correctly aligned and clamp the end blocks. Trace the inner contour of each side where it meets the soundboard. Pencil in around the linings and both blocks.

Clamp the workboard to the workbench and clamp the soundboard facedown in position. When laying down the soundboard, always make sure the surface is free of scraps or debris. Most of the woods used in guitar making are harder than the spruce top and an unnoticed speck of ebony can leave a serious, exasperating dent. Also avoid excessive handling of the soundboard to keep it as free as possible of oil, perspiration, and dirt.

Pencil in the positions of all major struts and braces. The large cross brace, or X-brace, is fitted first. This is the main structural support member of the soundboard and must be fitted with great care.

Mark off the position of the mortise on each brace. Cut out these mortises with dovetail saw and chisel. Work scant so that you have to enlarge the mortises gradually until the two cross members make a tight fit. The intersecting joint should fit without any gaps. If this joint is sloppy, much of the X-brace's effectiveness will be dissipated. This brace, as well as all the others, should be Sitka spruce sawn on the quarter and as stiff as possible. End grain should be vertical for maximum strength.

All gluing edges of braces must be square and level, with no unevenness or twists. Apply Titebond liberally and hold the X-brace in position for about twenty seconds. Position clamps and gradually tighten while making sure nothing has shifted.

Glue in the remaining braces, making sure that all their gluing surfaces are square and level. Chisel out the scooped ends after gluing, and bevel their edges. Smooth all the bracing with fine sandpaper.

68. *Clamping braces to soundboard*

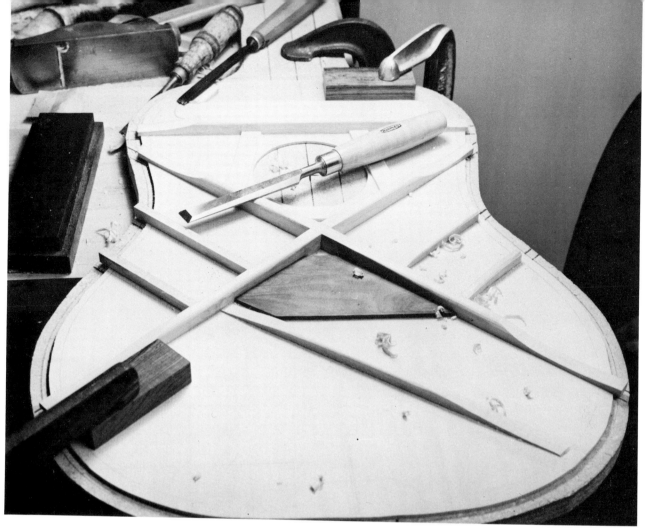

69. Partly chiseled bracing

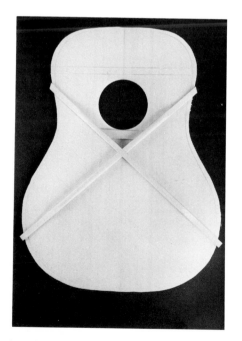 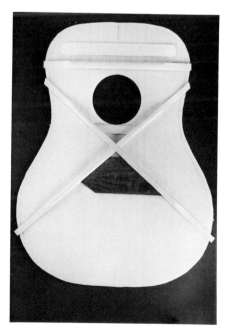 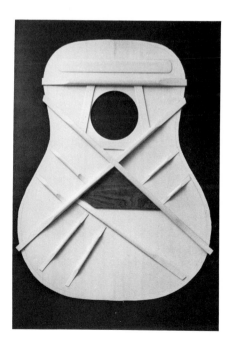

*70. Construction sequence for soundboard, all bracing
shaped except X-brace. Final shaping of the X-brace is
determined by the strength and rigidity of the top. A
strong top can have thinner bracing.*

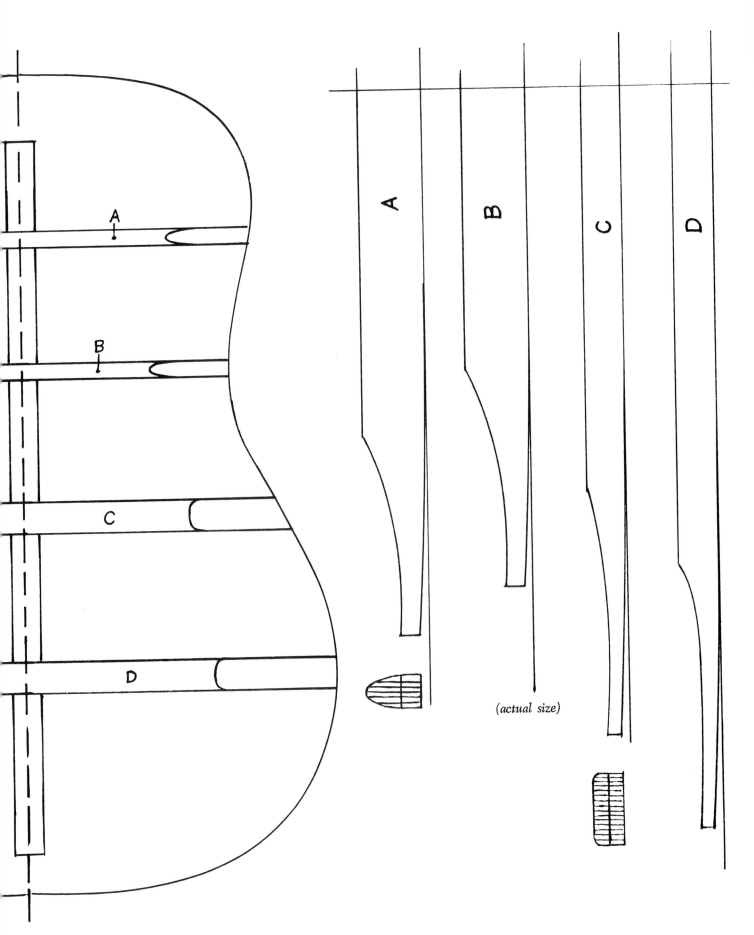

A

B

C

D

(actual size)

71. Plan of back

Back Construction

Jigsaw the back to shape and sand both sides smooth. Piece together strips of cross-grained mahogany and glue over the center seam. After gluing, bevel and sand smooth their edges.

The cross struts must be planed and sanded to the prescribed arch and carefully fitted in place. Openings are chiseled in the seam reinforcing strip for each of the struts. When gluing down the struts, beware of their shifting out of line when clamping pressure is applied. Use Titebond and wait half a minute until the tack starts to grab. Hold the struts in place with hand pressure while waiting and then apply clamps.

Now is the time to write in your name and the date.

72. *Clamping center strip*

73. *Sanding center strip with sanding stick and metal guard*

74. *Gluing arched struts*

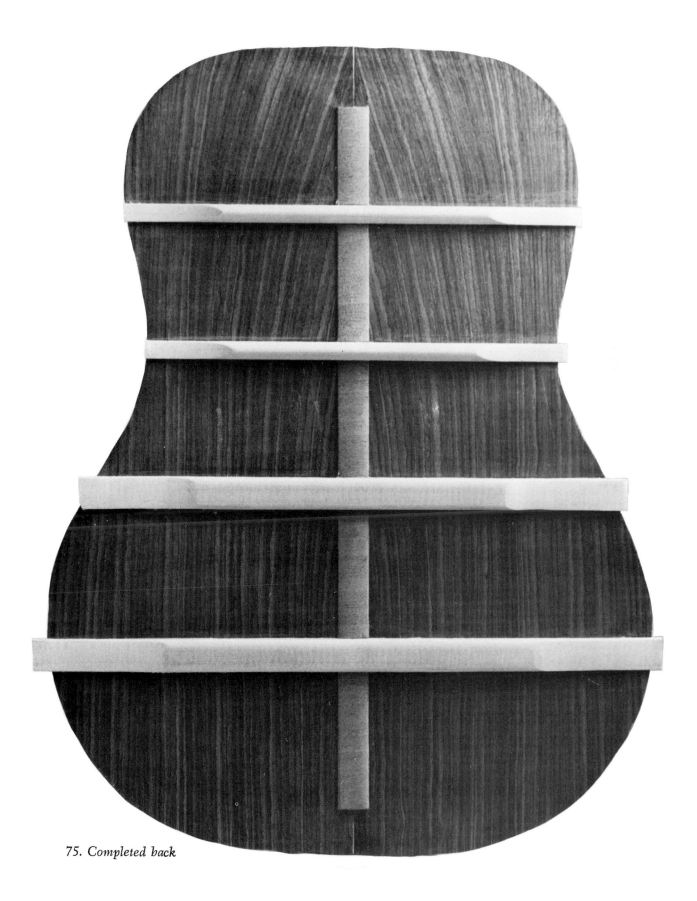

75. *Completed back*

Gluing Top and Back

With the side assembly in the mold, prop in place, lay the top down on the sides in position. Line it up exactly and place a weight on top so it won't move and you will have both hands free. Mark the cut-off point of the strut and braces that will be let into the linings to butt against the sides. Also mark the linings where they must be mortised.

Remove the top and saw off the ends of the strut and braces, observing the curve they must have to butt properly. Mark off the depth of each mortise and chisel the mortises out of the lining. Drop the top back into place.

Stretch a rubber band across the waist and invert the entire mold. Look through the holes and examine every part of the fit: linings, strut, braces, and both blocks. Remove the top and make whatever adjustments are required to ensure that everything fits. A common error in fitting top to sides is forcing the sides apart. Check the vertical face of the sides to make sure they have not been splayed.

Apply hide glue to the linings and blocks with a small brush. Lay it on with a patting motion to keep glue from leaking down the saw kerfs. Apply glue to all the mortised surfaces and to the outlined areas on the soundboard that will be glued. Press the top into place and secure all around with rubber bands. Invert the mold and clean out excess glue with a moistened brush.

Fitting the back is more complicated because of the arch. The sides must be pared down slightly, leaving the waist section slightly elevated. If you imagine the arc that the back makes across the lower bouts, you can readily understand why. The waist's narrower width requires that the sides be taller at that point to touch the arc.

Carefully plane down those sections that must be lowered. If the floor of the mold is dead level, a level can be used to make sure that both sides are uniform. The workboard can be placed on top of the sides to check on them as work progresses.

File all the gluing edges—linings and blocks—to a 2° angle. I use a homemade try square for this job. It is made from a single piece of $\frac{1}{16}$" brass and

76. Carefully marking position of braces on linings

two blocks of ebony. One blade is square and the other is pitched 2°. It is a convenient tool I use all the time.

With all the edges pitched 2°, fit the back and notch the linings, as was done with the top. This is the most exacting part of guitar assembly; proceed slowly, step by step until the back is comfortably seated. Stretch a rubber band across the waist and again invert the mold. Use a light and a flexible mirror to examine the interior fit of mortised joints, linings, and blocks. Before closing up the guitar make sure that all surfaces are clean and smooth. Roughness attracts dust and dust attracts moisture.

Glue the back on in the same manner as the top. Let dry overnight and trim all edges flush with the sides.

If the sides and back are rosewood or other open pored wood, wash coat, fill and seal before installing the purfling (see page 107).

77. 3½" try square

78. Checking back linings for correct angle

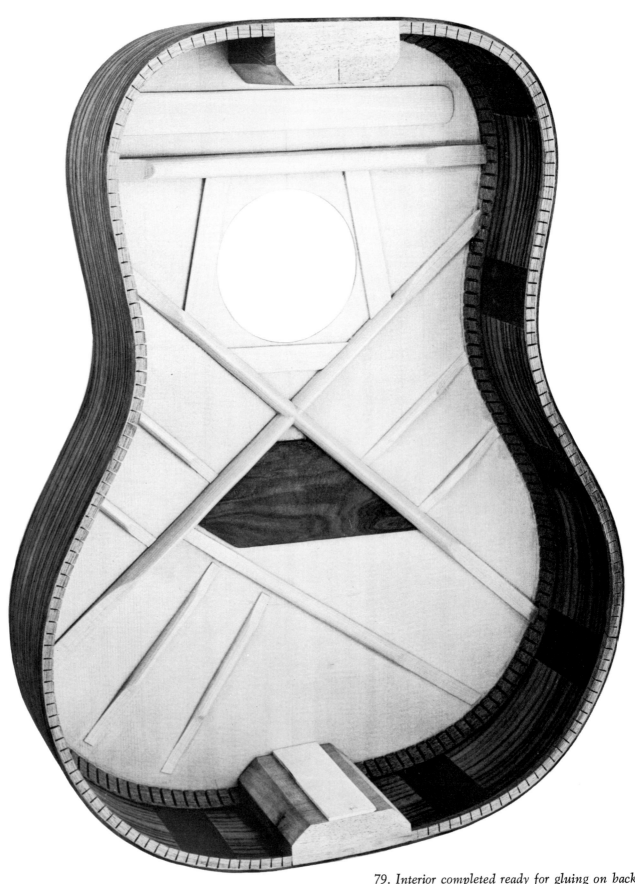

79. *Interior completed ready for gluing on back*

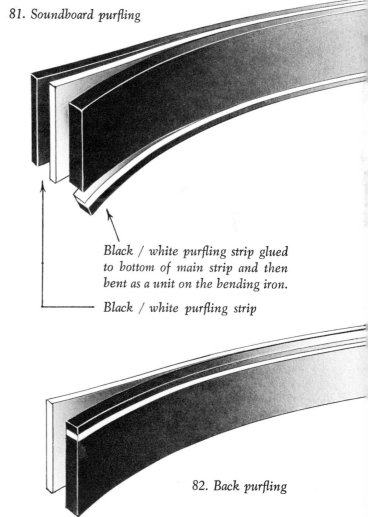

80. Purfling cutter in use

Purfling

Purfling, or binding, consists of alternating strips of dark and light veneers or plastic glued to a ledge cut into the leading edges of the guitar. Their purpose is to protect these edges and seal off the end grain of top and back.

In my guitars I use wood purfling because I prefer it to plastic. Plastic works fine; it is simply a matter of taste. Plastic bindings are quite flexible and do not require prebending, often necessary with wood purfling.

Before you cut the edge recess where the purfling will be glued, the top and back plates must be smoothed to a uniform thickness all around the guitar perimeter. Sand the top edge to ³⁄₃₂″, the back edge to ⁵⁄₆₄″. Gradation should be gradual and need not continue all the way up to the fretboard area, where vibration is minimal anyway.

Glue up a sample of the purfling you plan to install. Use this sample to adjust the purfling cutter to the proper width of cut. Test the cutter on a scrap board to make sure the cutter is set to the correct width. It is standard practice and prudent to cut the ledge a hair smaller than the purfling. It is easy enough to clean up the excess purfling with a scraper —a lot easier than scraping down the sides because the ledge was too wide.

With the cutter knife protruding about ³⁄₃₂″, make the first incision around the top perimeter. Keep the knife razor sharp and make the first cuts with light pressure, gradually increasing pressure as the

81. Soundboard purfling

Black / white purfling strip glued to bottom of main strip and then bent as a unit on the bending iron.

Black / white purfling strip

82. Back purfling

cut is deepened and less likely to throw the knife. The waist section, where the cutter is traveling along the grain, requires special care. Continue cutting until the correct depth is reached. Stand the guitar on edge and cut the sides. Hold the tool firmly with one hand and the guitar body with the other. Cut until the ledge comes away.

A herringbone or other wide inlay must be set into a separate ledge, which means cutting two distinct ledges. I did this with a router and carbide cutter set from Metropolitan Music Co. (see list of

83. *Jig for herringbone inlay*

suppliers in appendix). The ledges can be cut with a hand purfling cutter. Cut the top step first and then the side. For a first guitar it is better to use the one-step purfling and omit the side fillets.

Herringbone inlay is tricky to apply but the following method works well. Trace the template onto a board. Tape down waxed paper to cover the traced area. Drive small brads—spaced one inch apart—along a contour following the traced shape but ⅛″ inside it. Soak the inlay in very hot water for about one and a half minutes. Press the inlay up against the brad-formed contour and hold them in place with push pins. The inlay will probably fracture in ten places but it does not matter. Allow to dry on the form. Just before installation, dip the inlay into hot water for five seconds. Apply liquid hide glue to the ledge and bind in place simultaneously with the back-up purfling strip. Bind tightly with rubber bands and dry overnight. Do one half of the guitar at a time.

Wood purfling should be prebent on the bending iron to ensure easy and neat installation without fracture. White glue or Titebond can be quickly applied to the ledges with a plastic bottle that has a pointed nozzle to dispense a thin stream of glue. A scarf joint is the best method of concealing the bottom joint of wood veneer purfling; both ends are cut to a matching angle and overlapped. The heel joint can be butted because the heel cap is there to hold it permanently in place.

Plastic bindings can be installed simultaneously. Apply glue (see page 27) to the strips and ledge and hold bindings in place with rubber bands. Glue a small section at a time, binding and gluing as you go. Wipe away excess glue immediately because it dries quickly. The bottom joint on plastic bindings can be butted neatly on the center line because the solvent action of the glue will melt them together. They can also be joined in a scarf joint, the best way of finishing them if you are not using a solvent-action glue. Again, do only half the purfling at one time.

When all the purfling is done, glue in the inlay over the bottom center joint.

84. Scarf joint ending

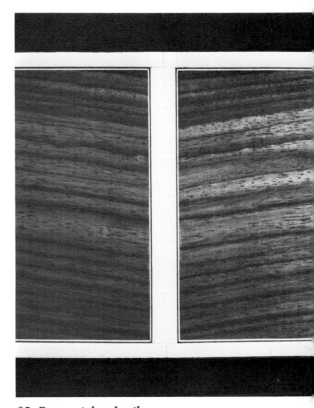

85. Bottom inlay detail

86. Traditional wrapping of plastic binding with ½" upholsterer's tape

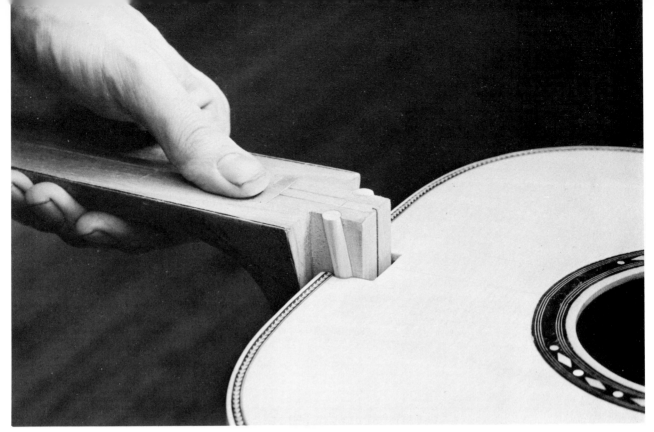

87. *Fitting doweled neck joint*

Joining Neck to Body

88. *Mortise cleaned out, shim in place*

Cut away the wood that conceals the neck block mortise. Start by making a hole in the soundboard and cutting away the spruce until the edge is flush with the mortise. Saw down the edges of the mortise and remove all the covering wood.

Place the body in the mold and remove the two L-hooks near the mortise. Clamp the mold to the workbench and set the neck tenon in the mortise. Place a prop under the neck so it is level with the soundboard. If the tenon protrudes on top, shave some wood off the bottom of the tenon; if the tenon is too low, glue a piece of veneer to the bottom of the tenon to bring the neck face exactly level with the soundboard. Stretch some rubber bands around the heel to hold the heel snug against the body.

Line up the neck so that the center line is straight from the nut down to the bottom of the guitar. This can be ascertained with a straightedge—metal or wood —or a string stretched between a tack at both ends. Set the bottom tack into the center line at the bottom

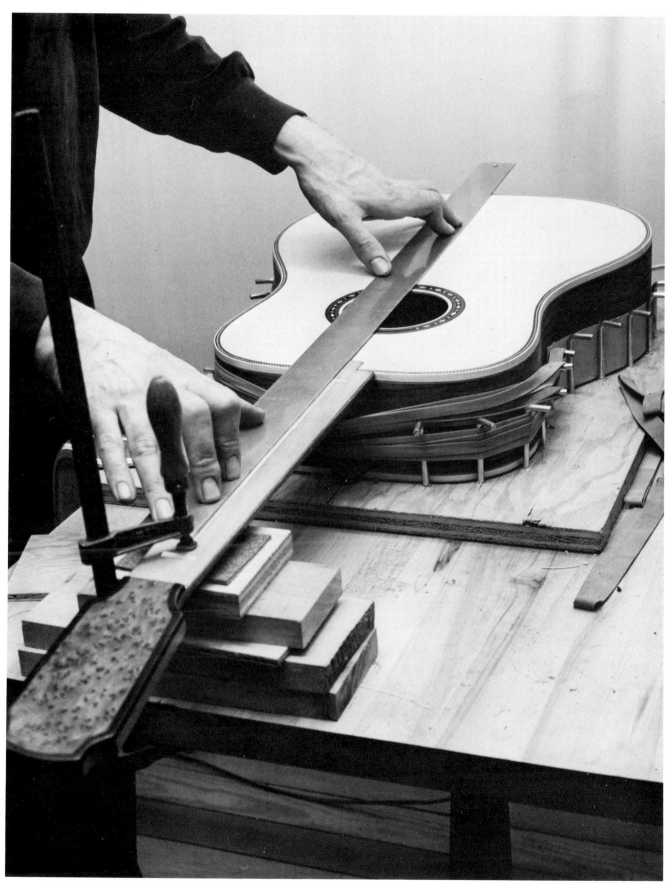

89. *Aligning neck before clamping*

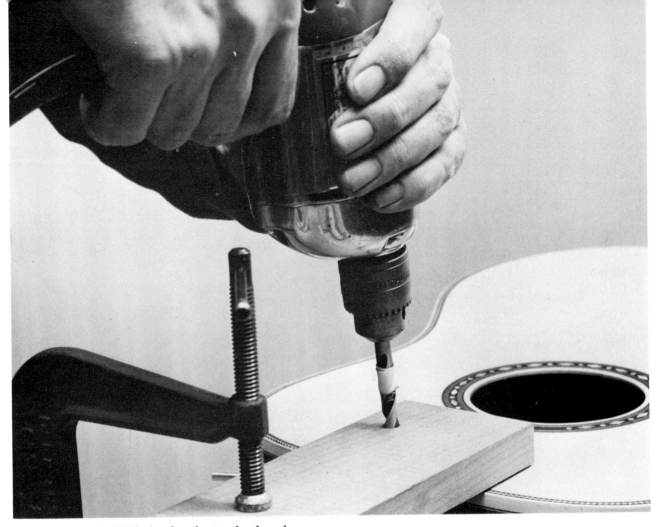

90. *Drilling angled hole for dowel using hardwood drilling guide. Note tape for gauging drilling depth.*

end of the mold. When the neck is centered, clamp it over the propped area.

If the neck joint looks good and the heel is tight against the sides, drill a ⅝₁₆″ hole straight down through the joint on each side of the tenon. Drill down at least 2″. Remove the neck and glue two ⅝₁₆″ dowels in the tenon grooves. Test the fit of the neck to make sure no obstruction will keep it from being properly seated. Saw a shallow groove vertically across the front face of the tenon; an escape channel for glue must be provided.

Glue the neck in place with white glue and clamp.

I use a variation of this method to ensure that the heel is jammed tight against the sides. Place a piece of veneer in the bottom of the mortise before fitting the neck. Drill the two holes at a slight angle

in toward the body. To ensure that the drill does not skew off into the neck block use a drill guide made of hardwood that actually angles the drill in toward the tenon. If the drill hole goes off into the neck block the dowels cannot be inserted until after the neck is glued, thereby forfeiting an important advantage.

Dowels slightly shorter than their grooves are glued in place and cut off flush on top. The veneer shim is removed from the bottom of the mortise. Clamping pressure will force the neck tenon down the extra thickness of the veneer shim, and the angle of the dowels will jam the heel in tight against the body. Clean up all squeeze-out and leave undisturbed for at least four hours.

After the neck joint is dry, cut and glue in place an ebony heel cap.

91. *Clamping neck joint, waxed paper under cauls*

92. *View of top joint and heel detail*

Bridge

Besides being an important link in the transmission of string vibrations to the soundboard, the bridge also affords an opportunity for artistic indulgence.

Bridge design is today a neglected area, but bridges can have many sculptural and decorative possibilities. Early guitar makers like Panormo, Lacote, and even C. F. Martin made highly individualized, stylized bridges that were as much a part of the guitar's identity as the body shape and head profile. Whatever distinctive qualities you can give to the design and character of your guitar will sharpen your own sense of pride and accomplishment.

Start by making sketches of design ideas. General dimensions of steel-string acoustic bridges run up to about $\frac{3}{8}'' \times 1\frac{5}{16}'' \times 6\frac{1}{2}''$. Make an accurate full-size drawing of your final design, allowing for saddle and bridge pins.

Both rosewood and ebony are used for bridges, the choice being entirely an esthetic one. The absence of grain or figure makes ebony a more attractive choice for carving and design effects that rely on sculptural qualities. Ebony does not have to be filled, will not bleed under solvent action the way rosewood will, and can be finished by simply buffing with wax.

The bridge of the guitar described in this book began with a block of ebony $\frac{5}{16}'' \times 1\frac{5}{16}'' \times 8''$. I jigsawed the back contour to shape and drilled a small hole in each corner of the block. Brads were then driven in securing the block to a rectangular workboard. I made saw cuts down through the block where each bridge arm ended. This saw cut did not go all the way through, but stopped about $\frac{1}{8}''$ short. All the rest was carved with chisels. The sharp corners

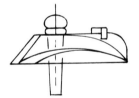

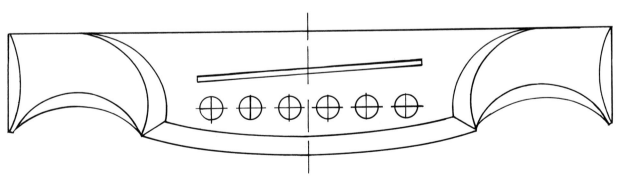

93. Bridge plan (actual size)

94. *Ebony bridge pins with pearl dot inlay*

and inner contours were smoothed with riffler files and sandpaper.

Mark off the positions of the bridge pins and saddle. Drill the pinholes to the size of the middle diameter of the pin you will use. Ream them to a tapered shape with a large rat-tail file. Keep testing the pin for fit and ream the hole until the pin stops about $\frac{1}{32}''$ short of being seated.

Scribe the position of the saddle with a pointed metal scriber and cut the outline of the groove with a sharp knife. Remove the wood from the saddle groove with a $\frac{1}{16}''$ chisel. Run the edge of the chisel back and forth like a scraper to deepen and level the channel until a $\frac{5}{64}'' \times \frac{1}{4}'' \times 2\frac{1}{2}''$ ivory or bone saddle fits snugly in the slot.

Stock bridges of the Martin type are available inexpensively from supply sources, but making your own unique bridge is not difficult. In the spirit of the guitar-making experience, I would urge that the novice builder try making his own bridge.

95. *A file tang polished on all four sides makes a good reamer*

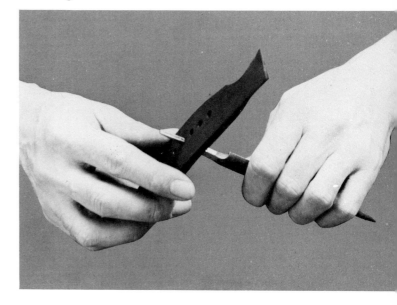

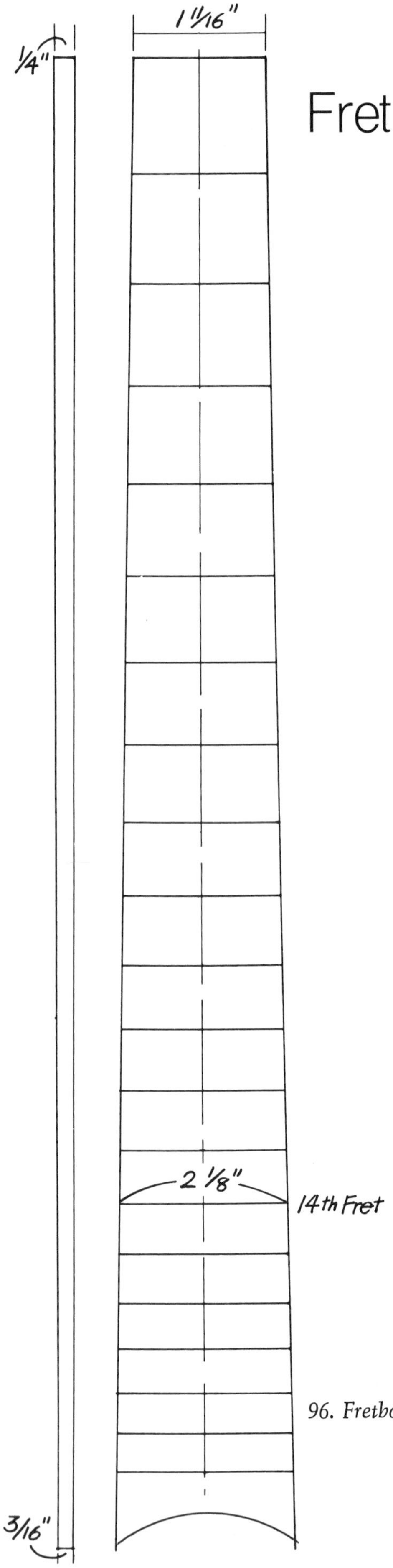

Fretboard

1 11/16"

1/4"

Drill a small hole in each corner of the fretboard and fasten it to a larger workboard with a small brad in each hole. Sink the brads well below the surface with a nail set.

Smooth this side of the fretboard dead level with scraper blade and long sanding block. When a metal straightedge shows that the surface is level, remove the brads and turn the board over. Replace the brads, sinking them below the surface.

Scrape and smooth the top to the bevel shown in the diagram. Steel-string fretboards are arched to a radius of 18" to facilitate the fingering of barré chords. Make a small template of wood or white plastic to ensure uniform arching over the length of the fretboard.

Traditionally, fret positions have been laid out to a formula known as the rule of the eighteenth. The vibrating string length is divided by 18 to locate the first fret. The remaining string length is again divided by 18 to find the second fret and so on. This formula contains a slight error because 18 is an approximate figure. The precise figure is 17.835, and the six-string and twelve-string scales listed here have been computed with this divisor. Both these scales, along with two classic guitar scales, have been produced on an accurately etched stainless-steel ruler (Ibex Fret Rule) available from suppliers.

Mark the fret grooves with a knife or pointed metal scriber against the edge of a try square. Saw the slots to a depth of 1/16" full with a backsaw or dovetail saw. A strip of masking tape or a block clamped to the saw blade will help gauge the depth of cut.

After sawing the slots, dress the entrance of each slot with a three-cornered file to remove the corner of each edge. Just one or two light strokes to dull the edges—no more. This will facilitate future lifting of the frets without chipping the face of the fretboard.

Pencil a line down the center of the fretboard, continuing onto the workboard. Locate the axis for scribing the circle where the bottom cuts off around the sound hole. Scribe the circle with dividers or compass. Draw the tapered sidelines on the fretboard.

2 1/8"

14th Fret

96. Fretboard plan

3/16"

SIX-STRING SCALE (25¹¹⁄₃₂″)
Fourteen frets clear of the body

Nut to fret		Fret to fret		Fret to fret (nearest ¹⁄₆₄″)	
1	1.423	1	1.423	1	1²⁷⁄₆₄
2	2.765	2	1.342	2	1¹¹⁄₃₂
3	4.032	3	1.267	3	1¹⁷⁄₆₄
4	5.228	4	1.196	4	1³⁄₁₆
5	6.357	5	1.129	5	1⅛
6	7.423	6	1.066	6	1¹⁄₁₆
7	8.429	7	1.006	7	1
8	9.378	8	0.949	8	⁶¹⁄₆₄
9	10.274	9	0.896	9	⁵⁷⁄₆₄
10	11.120	10	0.846	10	²⁷⁄₃₂
11	11.918	11	0.798	11	⁵¹⁄₆₄
12	12.672	12	0.754	12	¾
13	13.383	13	0.711	13	⁴⁵⁄₆₄
14	14.054	14	0.671	14	⁴³⁄₆₄
15	14.688	15	0.634	15	⁴¹⁄₆₄
16	15.286	16	0.598	16	¹⁹⁄₃₂
17	15.850	17	0.564	17	⁹⁄₁₆
18	16.383	18	0.533	18	¹⁷⁄₃₂
19	16.886	19	0.503	19	½
20	17.361	20	0.475	20	¹⁵⁄₃₂

SIX-STRING COMPENSATION:
from twelfth fret to bridge saddle = 12¾″

TWELVE-STRING SCALE (24²⁷⁄₃₂″)
Twelve frets clear of the body

Nut to fret		Fret to fret		Fret to fret (nearest ¹⁄₆₄″)	
1	1.395	1	1.395	1	1²⁵⁄₆₄
2	2.710	2	1.315	2	1⁵⁄₁₆
3	3.953	3	1.243	3	1¹⁵⁄₆₄
4	5.125	4	1.172	4	1¹¹⁄₆₄
5	6.232	5	1.107	5	1⁷⁄₆₄
6	7.276	6	1.044	6	1³⁄₆₄
7	8.262	7	0.986	7	⁶³⁄₆₄
8	9.193	8	0.931	8	⁵⁹⁄₆₄
9	10.071	9	0.878	9	⅞
10	10.900	10	0.829	10	⁵³⁄₆₄
11	11.683	11	0.783	11	²⁵⁄₃₂
12	12.421	12	0.739	12	⁴⁷⁄₆₄
13	13.118	13	0.696	13	⁴⁵⁄₆₄
14	13.776	14	0.658	14	²¹⁄₃₂
15	14.398	15	0.622	15	³⁹⁄₆₄
16	14.984	16	0.586	16	³⁷⁄₆₄
17	15.537	17	0.553	17	³⁵⁄₆₄
18	16.059	18	0.522	18	³³⁄₆₄
19	16.553	19	0.494	19	³¹⁄₆₄

TWELVE-STRING COMPENSATION:
from twelfth fret to bridge saddle = 12½″

Remove the fretboard, saw off the tapered side-pieces, and cut out the bottom semicircle. Sand the edges of the fretboard by running them over sandpaper.

Rest the fretboard on the neck and make sure it makes contact with the neck at all points without pressure. Check the alignment of the fretboard by placing two flat sticks or straightedges along each side of the fretboard. They should extend the length of the fretboard down past the bottom of the guitar. If the fretboard is properly aligned, the inner edges of the sticks will be equidistant from the center line at the bottom of the guitar. If the neck is properly aligned, the fretboard should be aligned automatically. If it is slightly off, you do have a small variable in the extra wood left on the neck.

Apply Titebond to the fretboard and to the area it will occupy on the guitar. Clamp and let dry overnight. After it is glued, finish off the neck flush with the edges of the fretboard.

Fretting will go smoothly if the slot is correctly sized to the fret wire. Unfortunately, suppliers do not stock a full range of fret wire gauges—about ten—but some carry thin, medium, and heavy gauge. Gauge refers to the thickness of the studded tang; the bead remains the same thickness, although fret wire with a wider bead is available.

In order to ensure that your slot matches the tang of the wire you are using, you must saw a trial slot in a waste section of your fretboard. Using another kind of wood won't work; the same slot will require a thicker tang in a rosewood fretboard than in an ebony fretboard because rosewood is softer.

Hammer in the test wire with an overhang of about ¼". It should go in with a few taps and stay there. Crimp over the overhang with a light tap; if the fret is loose it will rise in the middle. If the slot is too narrow, inordinate force will be required to anchor the fret, a dangerous practice because the accumulated wedging action of such fretting will bend a neck over backward. Wedge-fretting of this sort, in fact, is a standard repair technique for cor-

98. Sawing fret slots against try square

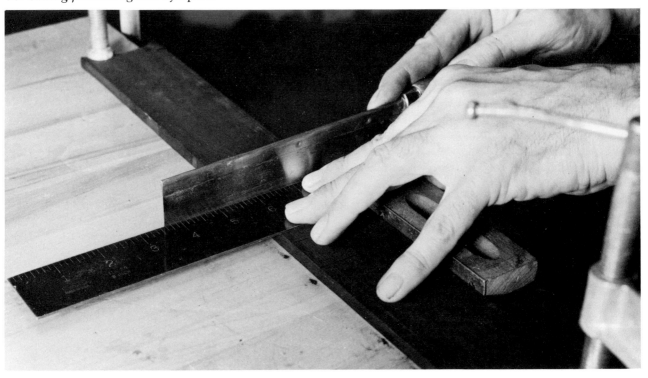

99. Aligning fretboard with two straightedges positioned an equal distance from center line at bottom

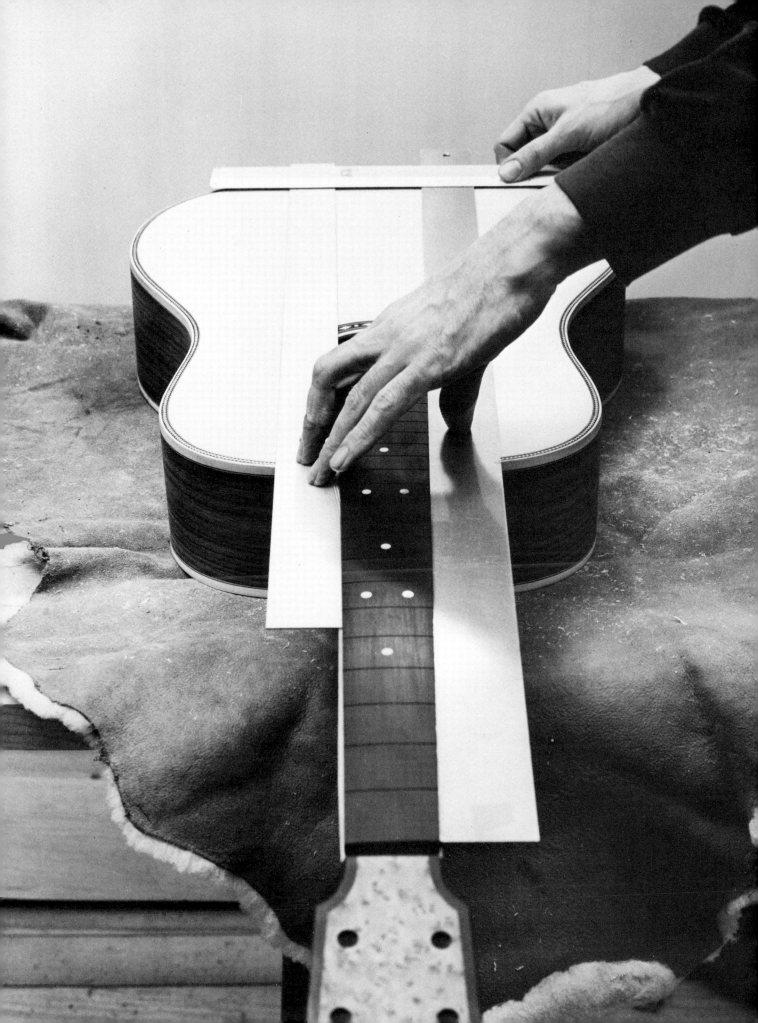

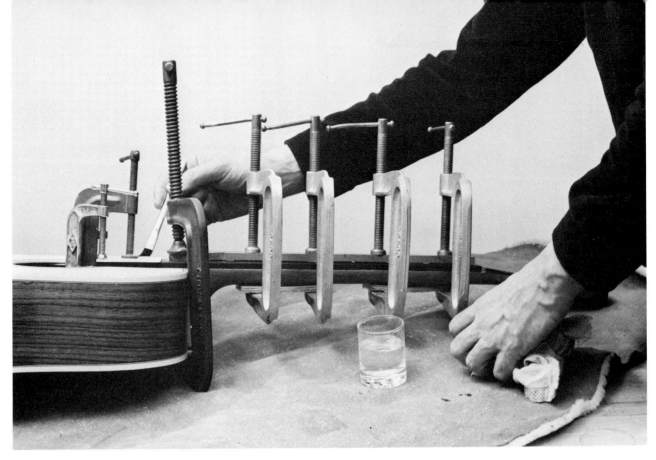

100. Fretboard clamped, cleaning out squeeze-out

101. A few drops of water will facilitate fretting

102. A few firm taps should anchor fret wire

recting neck bow.

There are three remedies for a loose slot: using a thinner saw, hammering or filing off slightly the set of your saw's teeth to make it thinner, or switching to a heavier gauge of fret wire. But take the time to achieve a proper mating of fret wire and slot.

The use of glue in anchoring frets is a matter of personal choice. If the tang and slot are right, glue is unnecessary. If glue is used, special care must be taken to make sure all the fret wire shoulders rest solidly on the fretboard. Glue ooze has a deceptive way of filling a narrow crevice, giving the impression that the fret wire is solidly against the wood when in fact it is not.

Cut all the frets beforehand, leaving about ¼" overhang on each end. Position each fret and drive it home with the polished, slightly rounded face of any medium-weight hammer. Do not use a fretting hammer for any other purpose. If the face of the hammer is dented or scarred, these marks will leave their imprint on the fret wire, which is relatively soft. Just a few firm taps will seat a fret. Use a hand-held support inside the body and under the fretboard when driving in frets near the sound hole.

Clip off all the ends with a flush-cutting nipper and file them flush using a 10" flat-mill bastard file.

File frets on the treble side from the head toward the body; on the bass side, from the body toward the head. Always file frets in a manner that tends to push them into the slot rather than pull them out. Apply strips of ¼" masking tape alongside each fret to protect the fretboard while you are filing the frets.

Gently glide a long carborundum stone or flat file over the tops of the frets. This will level out any remaining unevenness and leave a narrow, flat ridge on top of the frets. This ridge is easy to see because of the abrasions left by the stone or file moving over the frets. All filing and rounding of the frets is done with this flat ridge as a point of reference. As the sides of the frets are carefully filed and rounded, the ridge will gradually narrow and disappear. Each fret end is first beveled and then rounded off. Two files are usually used for dressing frets to their final shape— #2 and #4 extrafine pillar files. Finish off the frets with a worn piece of crocus cloth.

Inevitably, there will be gaps visible along the edge of the fretboard where the slot is deeper than the tang. Fill these holes by burning-in with a lacquer stick. Sticks come in many colors, and are applied with a heated knife or fine soldering tip.

Finish the fretboard with a light coat of refined linseed oil rubbed to a soft sheen with a clean rag.

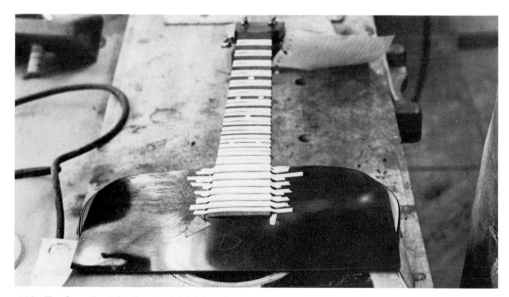

103. Fretboard with plastic shield in place to protect body while filing frets

104. *Bridge clamped in area delineated by masking tape to betray any shift while clamping*

Bridge Position/Compensation

Theoretically, the twelfth fret lies exactly halfway between nut and saddle; the harmonic octave of a string at the twelfth fret should respond in the same pitch as a fingered note at that fret. In actual practice this does not occur because of the increase in string tension caused by fingering, and to compensate for this added tension the bridge must be moved back slightly.

This movement is called compensation, and the amount of compensation varies depending on string mass and tension and on the degree of string displacement when fingered. Electric guitars that have an extremely low action, with strings so close to the frets that fingering causes little string displacement, need hardly any compensation. Acoustic guitars that have a high action suffer a more severe displacement and need a larger compensation, especially if the scale is a short one. The longer the scale or vibrating length of the string, the less need there is for compensation. Bass strings, in proportion to their increased mass, are more profoundly affected by string displacement, and steel-string guitar saddles are always slanted to compensate for this increase in string mass.

The fretting scales used on the guitar described in this book are listed with an average compensation for light to medium gauge strings. If the saddle is made about ⁵⁄₆₄″ thick, the rounded point that stops the strings can be shifted by reversing the saddle or making a new one with a repositioned stop point. This will give you a variable of about ¹⁄₁₆″ to play with if you need it.

Make sure the bridge is perfectly aligned and centered. Mark its position lightly with a sharp pencil. If the bridge is rosewood, wash the entire bridge with acetone or benzol. When the bridge is thoroughly dry, coat the top surfaces with a wash coat of shellac reduced one part white shellac to five parts alcohol by volume. A rosewood bridge must be filled and sealed before being glued in place. This is necessary to keep the rosewood from bleeding onto the soundboard, as it might if sealed after gluing (see section on finishing, page 106).

Sand smooth the bottom of the bridge and glue in place with white glue. Clean away surplus glue and leave clamped for a day. Drill the pin holes through the body and file the string grooves.

105. Face of completed guitar

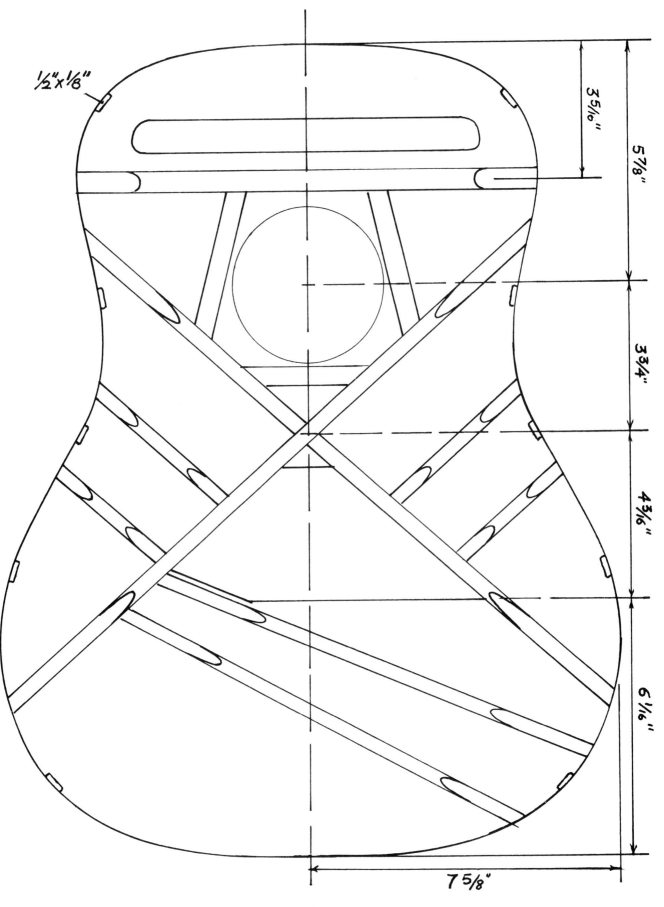

½"x⅛"

3 5/16"

5 7/8"

3 3/4"

4 3/16"

6 1/16"

7 5/8"

106. *Twelve-string plan*

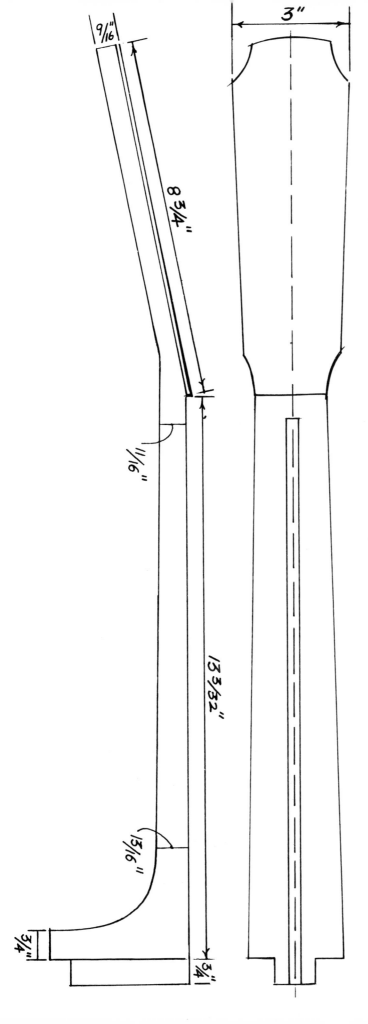

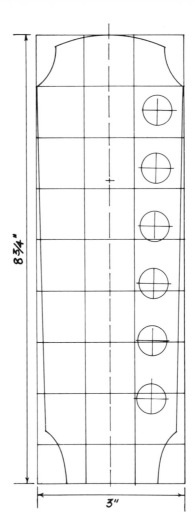

Twelve-String Guitar

Basic construction procedures are the same but there are important structural differences between six-string and twelve-string guitars. The added tension of twelve strings necessitates the following adjustments:

Neck: Quartersawn maple or cherry recommended with steel reinforcing bar or adjustable truss rod
Soundboard: ⅛″ thickness with edge taper to ³⁄₃₂″
Side braces of ⅛″ × ½″ spruce instead of cloth tapes
Larger reinforcing plate

A twelve-string neck is twelve frets clear of the body and uses a short scale for fretting (page 85) to lessen tension. The head must be elongated to accommodate twelve tuning machines.

93

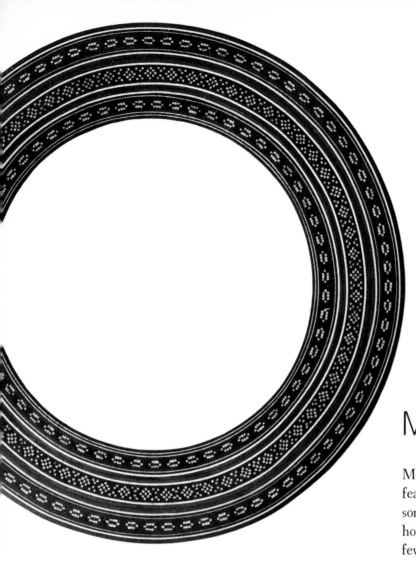

Mosaic Rosette

Mosaic inlay around the sound hole is a common feature of classic guitars. Early steel-string guitars sometimes had mother-of-pearl inlay around the sound hole, but the modern steel-string guitar has only a few simple strips of veneer encircling the hole. The custom guitar maker is not bound by the exigencies of business economics, and there is no reason why a steel-string guitar should not have a decorative rosette.

The complex appearance of the mosaic inlay belies the ease with which it can be made. To make a simple rosette takes only a few hours. Complex rosettes may take as long as eight to ten hours.

A mosaic inlay is made of a series of tiles sliced from a mosaic log. The log consists of a number of planks made of thin, square wooden sticks of different colors arranged to form a design.

Wooden strips for making rosettes are available $\frac{1}{32}''$ square, and come in white, straw, black, red, blue, and green; brown (rosewood) strips $\frac{1}{32}''$ square are too fragile to work with. The others are easy to work with and despite their seeming fragility, present no real problems in handling. For those afraid of

110. Gluing up planks

111. Sawing tile in small miter box

three are in place take the next strip and glue it to the outside of the tiles. This strip will serve as a retaining wall for the tiles as they are set in place. Stick push pins against this strip to hold the tiles against the inner strip. The water will have softened the glue holding the bits of mosaic together and permit squeezing the tile into a tight fit. Use the tweezers as a prod, pushing and coaxing the tiles into an unbroken pattern. It may happen that the tiles resist neat juxtaposition because of insufficient taper. Do not remove these tiles, but let them dry in place. Increase the taper of the log slightly by scraping again with the razor. Cut three more tiles, moisten, and glue them in place next to the first three. If they fit well, cut all the tiles and continue around the circle keeping the retaining strip tight all the way. The illfitting group of three can be concealed under the fretboard when the rosette is inlaid.

Strips for the banding can be cut from purfling strips. Thick bands will crack under the strain of bending them into a tight circle. This can be avoided by soaking them in hot water until pliable enough to bend into a circle without breaking. Clamp the ends with a spring clothespin where they intersect and put them aside to dry. The fine strips used in manufactured purfling can be easily separated by soaking them in hot water for fifteen minutes. Prebending these fine strips is unnecessary.

When the rosette is complete, lift the nails and free the Masonite circle. Sand or scrape the top of the rosette level. Cut the rosette loose from the waxed-paper backing and sand away any paper stuck to the rosette. Store the rosette between two blocks of wood until ready to install.

An 8″ log of average thickness sliced in ¹⁄₁₆″ tiles will make two rosettes.

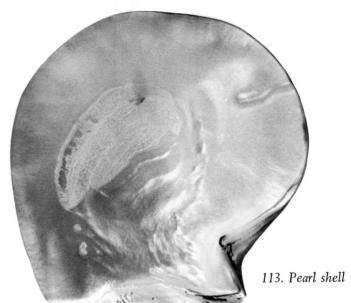

113. *Pearl shell*

Fancy Work

Guitars have been favored objects for decorative embellishment since the sixteenth century. Mother-of-pearl, ivory, tortoise shell, ebony, and other rare woods have been used to display the flamboyant talents of skilled craftsmen. Since the mid-nineteenth century, the classic guitar has been an austere exception, but the steel-string guitar offers a rich field of decorative possibility for craftsmen with an artistic bent.

Mother-of-pearl, referred to simply as pearl, comes from various marine bivalve shells of Indo-Pacific origin. Its color ranges from white to a pale golden hue.

Abalone, a marine univalve, comes from the Pacific and offers a richer, more variegated color range of pink, yellow, and greenish tones. Background pattern is more vivid, with darker contrasts than pearl. The two are often juxtaposed to make design use of this contrast. Pearl and abalone are sold in pieces up to about 1½″ × 2″ and about ¹⁄₁₆″ thick.

112. *Harwood guitar (ca. 1900) with pearl inlaid fretboard, paste and pearl purfling and rosette*

114. *Filling rosette groove with paste*

The pearl inlay rosette for my guitar is taken from the classic lozenge-and-ball pattern used by Stradivarius for the ivory and paste purfling of the Rode violin (1722). I began by cutting two Masonite discs, 4¾″ × 4³⁄₃₂″. The outer black and white rings were glued up around the larger disc, the inner rings around the smaller disc. When they were finished, they were removed and set in a groove around the sound hole sized exactly to accommodate them, about ½″ wide. Gluing the rings in place left a center channel ³⁄₁₆″ wide. The diamonds were cut from pearl and the 3-mm dots were purchased. They were glued in place at regularly spaced intervals with epoxy. A paste was prepared from refined charcoal tablets (drugstore item) and white glue. The tablets were pulverized in a glass using a screwdriver's plastic handle as a pestle. When the tablets were ground to a powder, enough white glue was added to give it the consistency of a thick paste. A small, thin spatula was used to spread and press down the paste in the spaces around the pearl inlay. After drying overnight, it was scraped clean and a second application of paste was necessary to fill holes and sunken areas. Final smooth-

115. *Abalone shell*

99

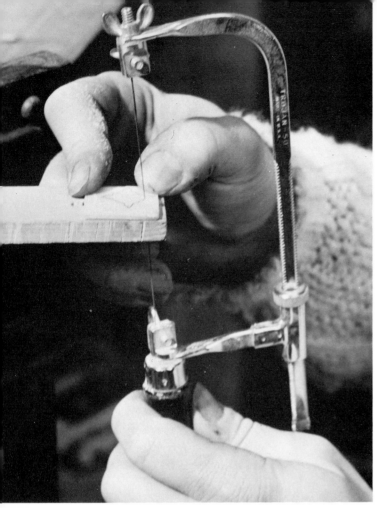

116. *Sawing pearl with jeweler's saw*

117. *Routing inlay area with Dremel tool*

ing was accomplished with a single-edge razor used as a scraper blade. An important point in making such a rosette is to have the pearl the exact height of the groove; it is much easier to sand the pearl before than after it is glued in.

Pearl is cut with a jeweler's saw using a fine blade (Herkules brand). These German blades come in a wide range of fine to coarse, and choice depends on the size and intricacy of the piece being cut. For most work #2/0 and #3 blades will serve. One end is secured in the saw frame—teeth raking down toward the handle—and then the saw frame is braced against the workbench to bow it in slightly. The other end of the saw blade is secured and the tension relaxed. Sawing is done with the blade stretched taut.

Sawing motion is almost vertical and must be maintained at an even, steady rhythm. The saw cuts only on the downstroke, and twisting or any abrupt turning of the fragile blade will snap it, especially if it is hot. Broken blades are commonplace in the beginning. When you can saw an entire piece without breaking a blade, you know you've arrived.

A great variety of pearl shapes—dots, squares, florals, snowflakes, and rococo design elements—are sold by some suppliers. They can be used as single elements or in combination to form larger designs, but are fairly expensive.

Before beginning an inlay, examine the pieces under a strong light for pinholes, fissures, and other flaws that might cause trouble.

Inlay starts with a design. For those luthiers short on design ideas, Franz Sales Meyer's *Handbook of Ornament* (Dover paperback, 1957) is an excellent source of inspiration and design material.

Draw on a sheet of tracing paper the design you wish to inlay. Prepare the pearl or abalone by sanding it smooth. Place the tracing on the pearl and trace it down with carbon paper and a 4H pencil. Spray the traced lines with two coats of Krylon crystal clear (art stores) to keep the carbon tracing from smudging while it is being handled.

A sawing platform must be made to facilitate sawing the pearl. The platform is a piece of wood about ¼" × 2" × 7". It is clamped to the workbench with about 4" projecting. A ½" hole is drilled in the middle of the overhanging projection and a channel is sawed to this hole to permit the saw blade to pass comfortably in and out. For very small pieces of inlay, the center hole may have to be smaller. All cutting is done over the hole, with the surrounding surface giving support for the inlay being sawed. Finger pressure is used to hold the inlay firm during sawing.

Saw out the piece carefully, blowing away pearl dust that may obscure the traced line. If filing is required to smooth roughly sawed edges, a small piece can be held in a wooden ring clamp with leather-faced jaws or a pair of parallel pliers. Dip the finished inlay in acetone or lacquer thinner to remove the spray and carbon tracing.

Place the inlay in position on the surface where it will be inlaid. Hold it down and trace its outline with a 6H pencil sharpened to a long, fine point. Success in inlay work depends on the precision with which tracings are made and followed by the saw. A Dremel motor drill in a stand is the best way of removing the major portions of the inlay mortise. A small router bit is lowered to a preset depth and routs away all but the sharp corners, which are cut by chisel. If you don't have a motor setup, you have to chisel out the mortise by hand. Incise the entire outline with chisels and then remove the waste wood. Exercise care when trying the pearl inlay piece for fit; twisting it while lifting it out of the mortise can break a delicate piece.

Inlaying can also be accomplished by sawing out the shape of the inlay in a piece of ¹⁄₁₆" veneer of the wood to be inlaid. The veneer is then glued down to the base wood and the inlay glued in place. Gluing is done with Titebond or 3M Scotch Super Strength adhesive. Small pieces of inlay can also be glued with a shellac stick of the wood color. The shellac is melted into the mortise with a hot knife or soldering tip and the pearl immediately set in place. Gaps in the inlay can be filled with charcoal paste or a shellac stick of matching color. Shellac sticks come in a great variety of wood tones and can be bought at paint stores that

118. *Two pearl inlaid banjo heads*

Top: A. C. Fairbanks Co. "Electric" banjo (ca. 1890)
Bottom: Lyon & Healy (ca. 1920), troubador composed of abalone and pearl

sell wood-finishing materials.

Large designs have to be made up of small rectangles of pearl or abalone carefully butted together. Matching of the pieces must be done in such a manner that the ensemble does not look like a series of butted rectangles. If the final inlay consists of pieces that are harmoniously juxtaposed to avoid a segmented appearance, it will look much nicer. When all the pieces are correctly arranged, they must be glued to a small panel of ⅛″ hard maple plywood (Constantine, see list of suppliers in appendix). After the assembly has been glued in place with Titebond, smooth the inlay surface with fine sandpaper. Trace down the design and saw it out. Soak off the pieces in hot water and reassemble them in the inlay mortise.

Pearl can be engraved with incised lines that can be filled with blacking to add design and textural interest to pearl inlay. Engraving is done with a graver and practice is necessary to gain control. Pearl is brittle and grainy because of its layered structure and making straight or curved lines on its surface is not an easy matter.

Hold the graver—lozenge or half-point cutter is best for pearl—with the handle in the hollow of the palm, with the bent fingers on the front edge of the blade with the extended thumb on the other side and the little finger fitting into the hollow of the handle. This is the traditional technique for wood engraving and also works for pearl although more pressure is

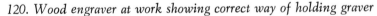

120. *Wood engraver at work showing correct way of holding graver*

119. *Banjo fretboard inlaid with engraved pearl, Vega-Fairbanks #7 (ca. 1910)*

121. Sawing elephant tusk for nuts and saddles

required. The main virtue of this method of holding and guiding the graver is that it gives great control because the thumb is always in contact with the surface being engraved. Curved lines are engraved by mounting the inlay on a block of wood and turning the wood as the graver cuts.

Holding the graver like a chisel and pushing it away from you leaves you without the control necessary to make designs of any intricacy and also presents the danger of slipping. A study of old pearl engraving reveals that the men who did this work were well versed in the traditional techniques of the wood engraver.

Lines can be blacked by wiping on black lacquer. When the lacquer dries, the top surfaces can be cleaned with a cloth moistened in lacquer thinner.

Ivory can be inlaid like pearl and was a popular material among seventeenth- and eighteenth-century luthiers. It is easier to engrave than pearl and will accommodate a finer line engraving technique. An old belief among luthiers is that pearl is more injurious to tone than ivory, which may account for Stradivarius' preference for ivory although pearl was easy to obtain in Italy.

122. Engraved ivory and ebony inlaid guitar, Joachim Tielke, Germany (ca. 1700)

123. *Decorative wood veneers for pick guards*

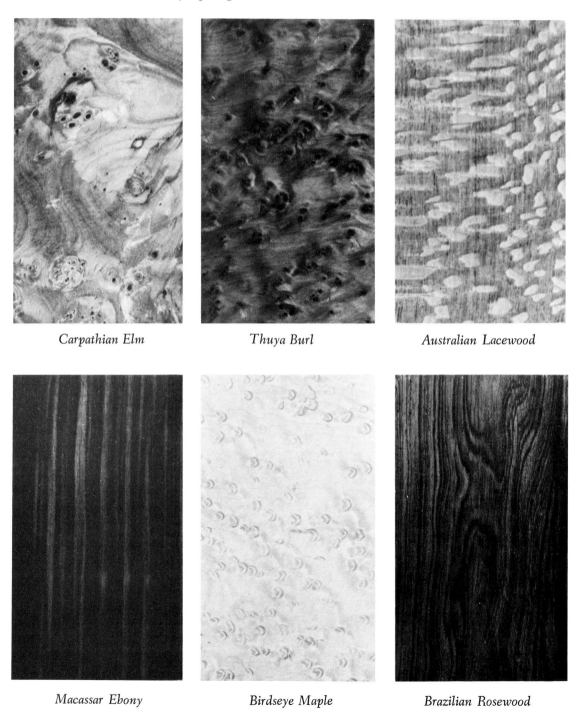

Carpathian Elm   Thuya Burl   Australian Lacewood

Macassar Ebony   Birdseye Maple   Brazilian Rosewood

Pick guards that are glued to the soundboard are usually made of flexible cellulose acetate material. They are cut in a great variety of shapes and sizes. Adhesion is accomplished with a special solvent that softens the surface to a gluing consistency. In a commercially made guitar the pick guard is applied before lacquering and lacquer is sprayed right over it. Custom builders usually apply the guard after the guitar is finished and polished.

The simplest way to attach a plastic guard to a finished, polished surface is with 3M Spray Adhesive. The adhesive is sprayed on the plastic, allowed to dry briefly, and then pressed into place.

Ready-made self-adhering pick guards with a peel-off backing are available from some suppliers. A problem with these as well as other plastic guards is that they tend to lift at the edges eventually or even to bubble in the middle.

Thirty years ago all flamenco guitars had a tapping plate made of maple veneer. Plastic was not used until after World War II. I like a wood veneer guard and use one now. Hardwood veneers come in a rich variety of grain patterns and wood colors. They are hard enough to resist pick damage and can be glued more effectively. Some of the most beautiful veneers seem no longer obtainable (amboyna, Circassian walnut), but plenty of attractive veneers are available: satinwood, curly maple, eucalyptus, lacewood, sycamore, and walnut.

When you have decided the shape of your guard, cut a pattern out of stiff cardboard. If you are using a plastic guard, place the pattern on top of a sheet of plastic and trace the contour several times with a sharp-pointed metal scriber. If scribing is done with enough pressure, the guard should break out easily along the scribed line. Sand smooth the contour of the guard and bevel the top edge with a scraper blade.

A self-adhering acetate guard must be cut to shape before the backing is peeled off. The area where it is to be affixed must be spotlessly clean. After the guard is cut out, peel back the backing to the middle of the guard and cut it across. Lift this loose piece of backing, move it slightly away, and stick it back down.

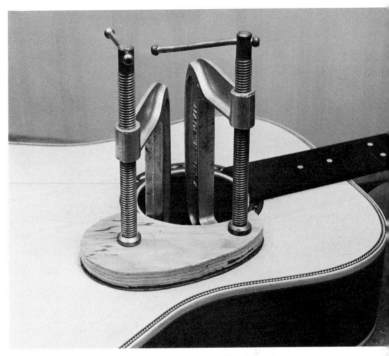

124. *Clamping veneer pick guard with fitted caul*

The guard is now covered with the backing except for a thin, sticky strip down the middle. Position the guard precisely where it is supposed to go and press down on the sticky strip. This will hold the guard in place while you peel off the backing. Start peeling from the sticky strip out, smoothing the acetate down as you go. Burnish the surface down until there are no air bubbles and every part adheres.

If you decide to use a wood veneer guard, lightly mark the position where the guard will glue on the soundboard. Prepare a wood clamping caul cut slightly smaller than the guard and lined with cork, rubber, or other resilient material to help distribute pressure. Coat the guard with Titebond and press down in place. Smooth it down and quickly wipe away all squeeze-out with a damp cloth. Clamp the caul in place and carefully remove all further glue squeeze-out. Leave clamped for at least four hours. Clean away dried glue and sand and finish with the rest of the guitar.

Finishing

A good finish enhances the appearance of a guitar by accentuating the beauty of the wood. More important, however, is sealing the wood to retard the absorption of atmospheric moisture and to protect against normal wear and tear. Unlike violins, guitars do not need fourteen coats of varnish. Heavy layering of lacquer or varnish on a guitar can, in fact, hurt the tone. No more finish need be applied than is necessary to seal and protect the surface properly.

Lacquer is in universal use among guitar manufacturers because of its rapid drying, a valuable attribute for mass production. Modern lacquers are made of nitrocellulose, resins, and plasticizers blended in a volatile solvent such as acetone, ethyl acetate, or amyl acetate. They are normally applied by spray gun in a fan-ventilated booth and are allowed a drying period of one to three hours between coats. Each coat must be thoroughly dry or the next coat will soften the finish down to the wood. Brush-on lacquers are available, but laying on a smooth coat with a brush is tricky because of the rapidity of solvent evaporation and the multisurface character of guitars. Sanding between coats of gloss lacquer (flat or matte lacquers are not used) is unnecessary because the solvent in each coat tends to soften the preceding layer, thereby effecting a good bond.

Lacquers are water clear and their visual effect on wood is minimal. Grain and color are intensified, but essential color or hue remains unchanged. Lacquer gives a tough, abrasion-resistant finish, but with less flexibility than varnish.

Oil varnishes for guitars and violins are made by cooking natural resins with oils, thinning with turpentine, and adding driers. Drying occurs through evaporation of the turpentine and solidifying (oxidation) of the resin-oil solution. The process of oxidation goes on for years and produces an extremely tough finish.

Varnish is a better choice than lacquer for the nonprofessional guitar maker. It can easily be applied

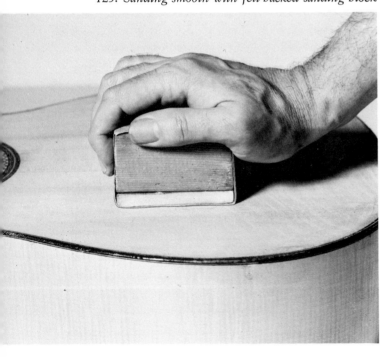

125. *Sanding smooth with felt-backed sanding block*

126. *Filling rosewood pores with filler mixed to cream consistency*

by brush, sparing the expense of spray equipment; it will not smell up the house as lacquer will; it will produce a more durable coating that can be brought to a lustrous finish with fewer coats than lacquer; and it will fill in and build up depressions as lacquer will not.

French polishing with shellac is another finishing process, but it is laborious and produces a finish easily marred by water.

White shellac remains the most popular sealer for use under varnish, while shellac-based sealers and synthetic sanding sealers are preferred under lacquer. Make sure your shellac is dated and less than six months old. Shellac, especially white shellac, must be fresh or it will not dry properly. If purchased in a metal can, store any remainder in a glass bottle as it may darken with age if left in a metal can that has been opened.

Spruce, maple, and cherry are close-grained woods and do not have to be filled. Open-pored woods such as rosewood and mahogany should be filled before finishing. Filler, a mixture of ground quartz silex

and pigment in a varnish-type vehicle, comes in several colors. The color of filler used should be the same or slightly darker than the wood it will fill.

To begin the finishing of your guitar, sand the entire instrument with 240 (7/0) garnet paper. Use a sanding block made of wood with felt glued to the bottom of the block. The felt slows the buildup of heat caused by friction and the clogging of sandpaper that heat can cause. It also prevents the gouging that can occur with a square block of wood.

Go over the soundboard lightly with a damp cloth to raise the grain. When dry, sand smooth a second time. Clean the surface with a tack rag, a rag impregnated with varnish until tacky but not damp.

Coat the entire guitar (except the fretboard) with a wash coat of 5-lb cut white shellac reduced six parts alcohol to one part shellac by volume. This preliminary wash coat makes the filling operation easier and gives cleaner results. It also prevents color changes in the wood by retarding the absorption of oils and resins contained in filler.

Sand smooth wash-coated areas with another light

127. *Wire hanger supports guitar while varnishing neck*

128. *Applying varnish*

going-over with fine garnet paper after the shellac has dried—an hour, usually.

Dig a lump of filler out of the can and thin it with benzine until it has the consistency of heavy cream. Brush it on parallel to the grain with a good bristle brush, working it into the pores. Avoid getting filler onto the spruce soundboard.

When the filler dries to a cloudy or fogged appearance—usually about twenty minutes—wipe off the excess filler with a coarse cloth. Remove the excess by rubbing across the grain with enough pressure to pad and pack the filler more firmly into the pores. Finish wiping by rubbing parallel to the grain with a soft, lint-free cloth. If the filler is wiped before it is sufficiently dry it will be pulled from the pores; if the filler is too dry, wiping will produce muddy results. Practice and good judgment will yield a professional job. On open-pored new wood, filling may have to be done twice to fill all the pores and provide a hard, smooth base for finishing. The final finish can be no better than the surface underneath.

Before any finish is applied to the guitar, the filler must be absolutely dry. Laying varnish or other coating on partially dry filler is a common finishing hazard. The final finish will not dry—necessitating removal of all finishing materials down to the wood and starting all over again. Allow at least a day, preferably two, for drying filler.

When dry, coat the filled areas with a sealer coat of 2-lb cut shellac made by mixing one part alcohol to one part 5-lb cut shellac. Allow overnight drying before lightly sanding with 6/0 garnet paper. When thoroughly dry, shellac will not adhere to sandpaper, but will leave a fine white powder on the surface. Gummed-up sandpaper means the shellac is inferior or that humidity has slowed the normal drying action.

A good varnish for guitars is tough, flexible, and clear. It should flow well, possess good self-leveling ability, and take at least a day to dry. Quick-drying varnishes are not suitable for stringed instruments, mainly because driers used in such varnishes tend to shorten the life of the varnish. My own preference in

108

varnish is S & W Varnish sold by J. F. Wallo and Luigi Nicoseco Oil Varnish sold by International Violin Co. (see list of suppliers in appendix). Follow the seller's recommendations for thinners and drying time.

Apply varnish with a soft-hair 1″ flagged and tipped brush. Shake dirt and loose hairs from a new brush by whipping it across fingers, twirling between palms, and tapping vertically on a flat surface. I use a red sable 1″ brush purchased in an art supply store for about fifteen dollars. It is an expensive brush, but I've had it about seven years and it will last me the rest of my life. It is never used for anything but varnish and is carefully cleaned in acetone, washed with soap and warm water, and dried after each using.

Apply varnish in long, even strokes with a minimum of brushing. Varnish the soundboard first. A clean, dry rag stuffed under the sound hole will keep varnish from dripping into the interior. Varnish the inner edge of the sound hole. Work under a good light to make sure no spot is left unvarnished. When the top is done, stand the guitar upright on some newspapers and varnish the sides. Supporting the neck with one hand, begin at the heel and varnish the sides as far down as you can go on the lower bouts. Suspend the guitar with a wire hook made from a coat hanger and finish varnishing the bottom section of the sides. Hold the neck and varnish the back. Steady the guitar while varnishing the head, neck, and heel by hooking your forefinger through the sound hole in back of the fretboard and pressing your thumb against the face of the fretboard.

When the varnish is dry, sand lightly with fine sandpaper—varnish does not adhere well to a glossy surface. Apply three coats, sanding between each coat. Before applying the fourth and last coat, sand away all bumps caused by dripping and overlaps.

The varnish should dry for two weeks—the longer the better—before being rubbed to its final polished finish.

First, smooth varnish with 400A wet-or-dry silicon carbide paper and water. Dip a folded piece of the paper into water and carefully smooth away all

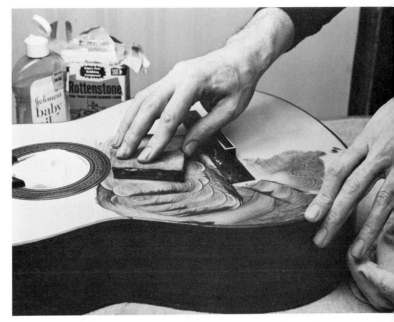

129. Rubbing varnish to soft gloss finish with felt pad, rottenstone, and mineral oil

lumps and unevenness. Inspect the surface frequently to avoid going through the finish. After initial smoothing has been accomplished, change to 600A silicon carbide paper and polish out all surface scratches. Use enough water to lubricate and float off the pulverized finish while polishing in a small, circular motion. Clean off the surface with a dry cloth and inspect frequently as polishing proceeds. Be extra careful when sanding the edges, the easiest places to go through the finish. This polishing operation softens the varnish, and final rubbing must be delayed for a few days. Powdered rottenstone and water rubbed with a felt pad will give the surface a high luster.

For a lacquer finish, seal wood with a synthetic sanding sealer or shellac-based sealer. In all cases follow manufacturer's recommendation as to sealer for his particular lacquer. Shellac used as a sealer under a lacquer finish must not exceed a 2-lb cut (2 lb of shellac to 1 gal of alcohol). A heavy shellac sealer may cause checking of the lacquer finish and may prevent some lacquers from drying at all.

H. Behlen & Brothers (see list of suppliers in appendix) market a lacquer—Qualatone #317—that contains fossil resins and is flexible enough for use on guitars. Load the brush with as much lacquer as it can hold and flow it on in one direction. Allow at least

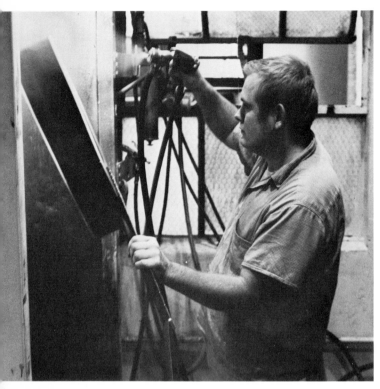

130. *Spray booth application of lacquer (C. F. Martin & Co.)*

131. *Buffing lacquer finish to high gloss (C. F. Martin & Co.)*

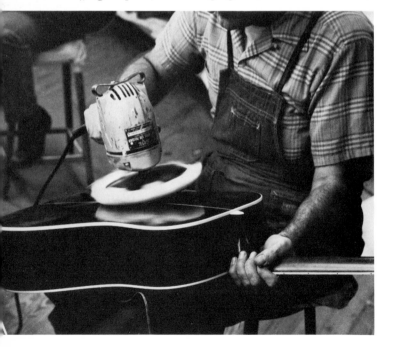

four hours drying time; sanding between coats can be confined to eliminating bumps and unevenness. Some luthiers use a scraper blade to smooth a lacquer finish between coats.

For spray-gun application of lacquer, pressure—normally about 45 lbs—must be adjusted to suit the viscosity of the lacquer. Spraying distance is usually about 10″. Too close spraying can cause sagging or pebbling known as orange peel. Spraying from too far at high pressure can cause a rough, sandy surface. Only experience will bring facility with a spray gun. Five or six coats of lacquer should suffice.

The final coat should be allowed to dry for a few days before final rubbing is attempted. Water and pumice rubbed with a felt pad will give a clean, clear finish. For a high-gloss finish, follow this rubbing with a lacquer-rubbing compound applied with felt pad in a circular motion. The same effect can be had by using a lamb's-wool buffer in a hand electric drill. Use Dupont #7 auto-polishing compound with the buffer to produce a high gloss.

Sunburst effects can be done only with a spray gun. A spirit varnish (alcohol solvent) of dark color is sprayed around the edges in a soft shading effect, and clear varnish is applied over it. H. Behlen & Bro. market staining colors miscible with French polishes and lacquers under the name Match-O-Stain. They also market an excellent padding lacquer, Qualasole, that has largely replaced the old French polishing technique using refined, de-waxed shellac.

A small pad of lint-free cotton or cheesecloth is shaped to a comfortable size for the hand. The pad is dipped into the Qualasole and then pressed against the palm of the other hand to ensure equal dispersion. Room temperature must be at least 65° F., the warmer the better.

Move the pad in circular or figure-eight motions, beginning with light pressure and increasing as the pad dries out. Slide the pad on and off the surface without stopping. Resting the pad in one spot will mar the finish. Do not use too much lacquer at one padding and allow at least an hour's drying time between paddings.

Stringing Up

Attach the tuning machines and string your guitar with light or medium gauge strings. To adjust the action, tune the guitar up to pitch (A440). If you are accustomed to tuning your guitar to a lower pitch, the action will have to be set accordingly.

Action refers to the quality of a guitar's playability and is determined by the distance of the strings from the frets and string tension. For an average action the distance of the treble strings at the fourteenth fret should be between $\frac{5}{64}''$ and $\frac{6}{64}''$. On the bass side the distance should be between $\frac{7}{64}''$ and $\frac{8}{64}''$.

For an action that is too high, lower the bridge saddle a bit. If it is too low, try a thin shim of veneer under the saddle. If this works, remove the shim and cut a new saddle to the right height.

If your soundboard is a strong, fairly rigid one you may find that light gauge strings will produce a tone lacking in fullness. This can be remedied by thinning the soundboard bracing Reach in with sandpaper and sand down the X-brace first. Proceed gradually, taking off a little at a time and then stringing the guitar to check the sound. Suck up sawdust by inserting a vacuum hose into the box.

Beware of weakening the braces too much. This procedure is not recommended for factory guitars unless you have a lot of experience in judging the inherent strength of a soundboard. Many good guitars have been ruined by zealous amateurs thinning the braces on soft soundboards that need strong bracing.

New guitars need to be played for several months before they begin to show their true tonal character.

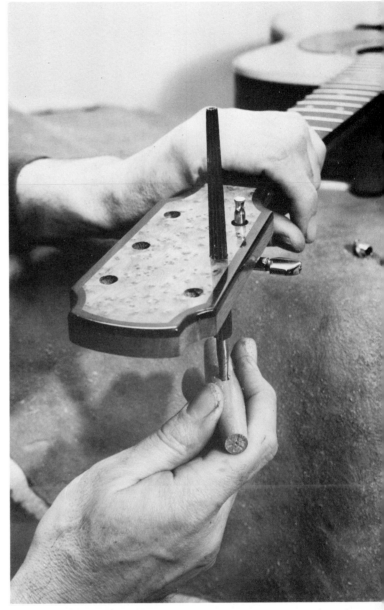

132. Reaming tuning machine holes for press fit (Schaller mini machines)

133. Nuts with string spacings (actual size)

$1\frac{11}{16}''$ *six-string*

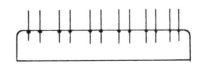

$1\frac{7}{8}''$ *twelve-string*

D'Aquisto Makes an Arched-Top Guitar

John D'Angelico was trained as a violin maker, but discovered—as perhaps Orville Gibson did—that buyers for new violins were scarce because old violins (even bad ones) were more prized and were easily obtainable. Making arched-top guitars was a logical step for him.

D'Angelico took the old Gibson L5 as his model and set up shop on Kenmare Street in Manhattan's Lower East Side. The high quality of his instruments gained him a reputation among professional musicians, and his shop became a gathering place for top-rank guitarists such as Tony Mottola, Les Paul, Chet Atkins, Jim Hall, Chuck Wayne, and Joe Puma.

D'Angelico died in 1964 after a career in many respects similar to Orville Gibson's. He was guarded, sensitive, and like Gibson remained a bachelor. Though shy, he would open up with people he trusted. He lived over his shop in the neighborhood

where he grew up, never made much money, and his idea of a good time was a stroll up Fifth Avenue.

The sole heir to his knowledge about the construction of arched-top guitars is James D'Aquisto, son of a tool-and-die maker who taught him a love of fine craftsmanship. In 1952, at age seventeen, D'Aquisto began taking guitar lessons. A friend who knew of his interest in the guitar invited him to go downtown and meet a famous guitar maker. The meeting with D'Angelico determined the course of D'Aquisto's life; he accepted a job as an apprentice guitar maker.

Over the next twelve years, until D'Angelico's death, D'Aquisto studied and absorbed all that D'Angelico could teach him. D'Angelico was not a hard master, but an impatient one. He disliked giving an instruction more than once, but D'Aquisto was an apt pupil and learned quickly.

134. James D'Aquisto chiseling mortise for neck joint

135. D'Angelico guitar

136. John D'Angelico at work (1945)

It takes D'Aquisto six to eight weeks to make a guitar, and his backlog of orders always stretches two years ahead. His skill as a maker of arched-top guitars has gained him an international reputation in a field where he has no serious competition.

Wood for a D'Aquisto guitar comes from the Austrian Tyrol. He buys only the best grade of spruce and curly maple, the same wood used in the construction of fine cellos. Running out of wood is one of his recurrent concerns, and he stockpiles all he can afford.

Soundboards and backs come to D'Aquisto roughly contoured to his specifications—an overall thickness of about ½". He carves both plates to their approximate shape, leaving enough wood for final carving after the body is assembled. The inner surfaces are carved and smoothed to their exact shape with round-bottom plane, scraper blades, and sandpaper.

The ⅛" × 2½" sides (dimensions are variable depending on tonal and loudness requirements) are

137. *Carving back with round-bottom plane*

138. *Checking thickness with clock caliper*

bent on an electric bending iron, a tricky job because of curly maple's erratic grain and the acute curve of the cutaway section. Surface fractures and scorching are common hazards; breaks are glued tight and scorching is easily sanded away. With the sides in the mold, neck and tail blocks of Honduras mahogany are glued in place, and kerfed mahogany lining is then installed. Thin side braces ½" wide are installed at 4" intervals around the sides.

After the f-holes are jigsawed out, the soundboard is accurately positioned on the sides locked in the mold. A small hole is drilled through each end of the soundboard for a brad driven into the blocks to hold the soundboard in place. The entire assembly is turned over and the contour of the blocks and linings is traced onto the underside of the soundboard. This done, the brads are removed. The same procedure is followed with the back.

Interior bracing of the top is accomplished with one major X-brace. D'Aquisto is extremely meticulous about the fitting of this brace, a task made difficult by the undulating character of the soundboard surface.

139. Marking f-holes for jigsawing

141. Scraping gluing edge to exact contour

140. Tracing arc onto X-brace member, pencil held steady, fingers resting on soundboard

116

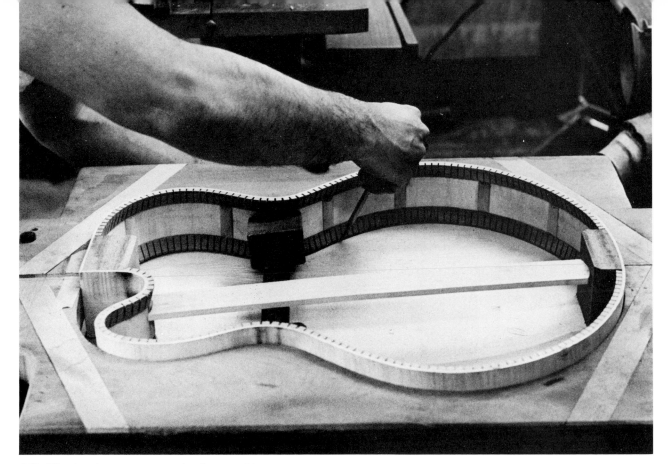

142. *Tracing inner contour of side assembly onto soundboard*

143. *X-brace resting on soundboard*

He bridges the surface with one spruce brace and—using a finger as a guide—he traces the soundboard contour onto the brace with a pencil. He jigsaws out the waste and then fits the brace. Endless shaving with a scraper blade and checking for fit continue until the bottom of the brace makes contact at every point with the twisting surface of the soundboard. The other brace is fitted in like manner.

When both braces are perfect, they are notched for their midsection joint. Mortising is done with the same precision. The cuts are made with a fine dovetail saw, and the waste is removed with a chisel. Fitting proceeds slowly with scraper and file until the joint is a gap-free force-fit. At any point in the operation, D'Aquisto is prepared to abandon an ill-fitting member and start fresh. He considers the fitting of the X-brace one of the crucial stages in construction and will settle for nothing less than a perfect fit. Titebond is applied to the joint and gluing edges of the brace. Clamps are fastened, and squeeze-out is care-

fully removed with a moistened bristle brush. When dry, the X-brace is rounded to final shape and cut off at the ends so that they stop short of the linings.

Black and white plastic strips are glued to the edges of both f-holes and scraped flush. Gluing of first the back and then the top to the sides in the mold is done with a clamping jig. The box is complete now with the plates overlapping the sides by about ⅜″. Rough trimming of the overlap is done on a band saw and then finished off flush with a rasp file.

Thumb pressure and tapping are the means D'Aquisto employs to establish the final thickness of the top and back. He carves and scrapes until the resistance of the surface to thumb pressure plus the sound produced by tapping tells him the thickness is right. Rough estimates of these thicknesses for the soundboard are ¼″ under the bridge, ⅛″ for the shallow depression around the edge, and ³⁄₁₆″ for the edge. The back is made slightly thinner because it is made

144. X-brace clamped in position

145. Plastic f-hole bindings scraped flush with top

146. *Clamping jig for gluing top and back to sides*

147. *Final thickness of top determined by thumb pressure and tapping*

119

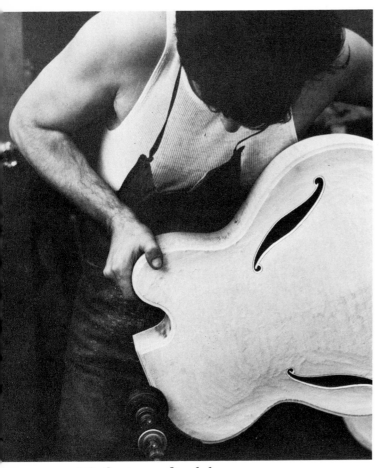

148. *Cutting purfling ledge*

149. *Clamping truss rod covering strip and head cheeks*

from much harder wood.

Binding ledges are cut with a special shaper with adjustable shims and bushings to regulate the depth and width of cut. The shaper or cutter is designed to avoid the problem of the curved surfaces, but much depends on D'Aquisto's skillful maneuvering of the guitar body against the cutter. The binding ledges are cut into the deep incurve of the cutaway section with a hand electric drill fitted with a small cutter bit.

Strips of black and white cellulose plastic are glued in place simultaneously, bound in the traditional manner.

The neck is cut from a block of domestic curly maple, preferred by D'Aquisto because it is harder than the European variety. The head is faced with ebony veneer and edge-bound in plastic like the body.

A curved channel is routed into the neck to accommodate the truss rod. A rounded entry is cut into the head where the adjusting nut sits. The extension of the neck that fits onto the body is a separate piece dovetailed onto the base of the neck.

D'Aquisto is a firm believer in adjustable truss rods, and his guitars are built to withstand the tension of a wide range of string gauges. A ³⁄₁₆″ drill rod is threaded at the top end, the other end is bent over and inserted into a hole drilled through the neck face into the heel. The adjustable nut works against a heavy half-round metal plate. When the rod is in place, a strip of maple cut to the curved shape of the channel is glued in place, keeping the rod down in the middle. If the neck bows, a twist of the adjusting nut will bring pressure to bear on the center portion of the neck, forcing it back into line (38).

The fretboard is glued on and slightly rounded with sandpaper, and a small ledge is routed on the leading edges for black and white plastic strips. Fret slots are cut and fret wire laid in. D'Aquisto uses two scales, 25¼″ and 25½″, depending on action preference of the buyer. After fretting is done, the edges are bound with a finishing strip of plastic.

Pearl inlay is let into the head facing and fret spaces, and the back of the neck is rounded with rasp and sandpaper.

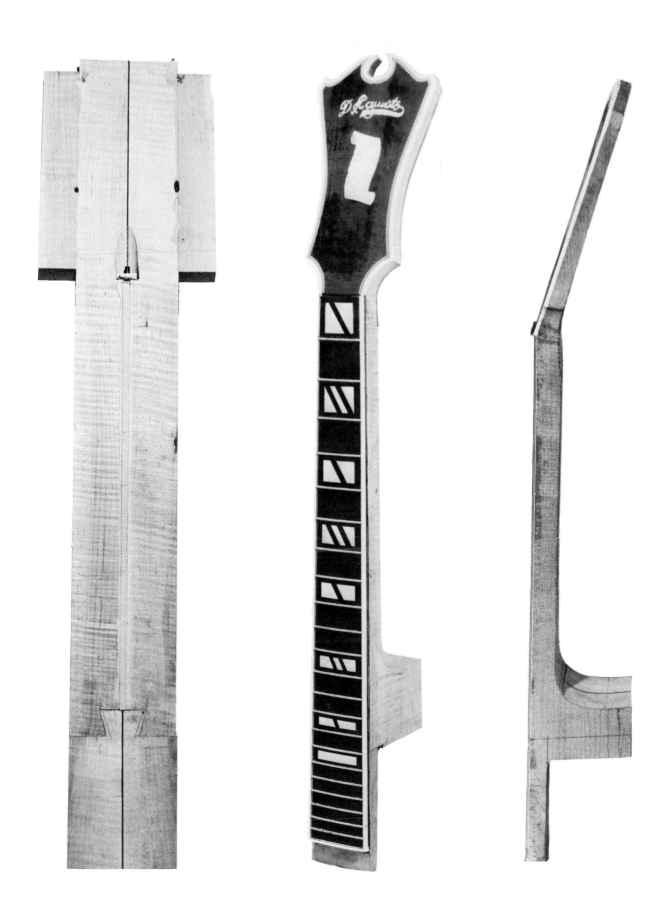

150. Neck at various stages

151. Sawing sides of mortise before chiseling

153. Final check for fit

152. Neck joint precisely fitted ready for joining

D'Aquisto then proceeds to the most difficult job of all: cutting the neck dovetail and body mortise for a precision fit of all contact surfaces when the neck is joined to the body. Like a violin's, the neck is raked back from the body at a slight angle. The dovetail is cut first. The heel shoulder in back of the dovetail is cut in at a slight angle so the shoulder will "bite" the sides when the neck is joined. It also leaves a small escape channel for glue squeeze-out. D'Aquisto once joined a neck to the body without leaving this exit, and the neck locked ½" short of being seated. Efforts to undo the neck joint resulted finally in cracking the body, a traumatic episode that still makes him wince. The escape channels are concealed by the heel cap.

The neck is fitted to the body and alignment is

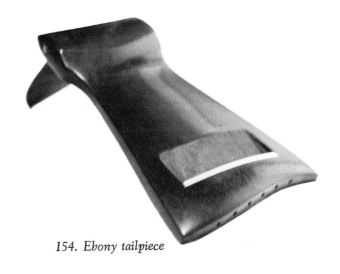

154. *Ebony tailpiece*

155. *Checking neck angle*

156. *Neck joint clamped, cleaning out squeeze-out*

Dimensions of D'Aquisto New Yorker:

Body length: 21½″
Upper bout: 13½″
Waist: 11¼″
Lower bout: 18″
Depth of sides: 3⅛″ to 3⅜″

accomplished with the aid of thin veneer used as a shim. When the neck is seated securely in proper alignment, it is glued in place and clamped. Squeeze-out under the neck projection is cleaned out with a cloth.

Excess purfling is trimmed with a scraper, and the entire body is smoothed with sandpaper.

The pick guard, bridge, and tailpiece are made of ebony. D'Aquisto abandoned the metal tailpiece because of its adverse effect on tone. He favors ebony with the natural, pale streaks left undyed.

Two coats of clear lacquer go on the guitar (sprayed) and then a body toner of colored lacquer. The toner is then scraped off the bindings with a small scraper blade. Nine coats of water-thin lacquer are sprayed on, and the surface is smoothed with 400-grit wet-or-dry paper. Final polishing is done with lacquer-rubbing compound and a buffing wheel. On blond guitars the toner coat is omitted.

Building the guitar is not the end for D'Aquisto. His customers, mainly famous jazz guitarists, have very explicit ideas about the kind of sound they want. Unlike builders of flat-tops and classic guitars, D'Aquisto has an uncanny degree of control over the tonal quality of his guitars after they are finished. By changing the bridge thickness he can influence balance: a thinner bridge will boost the treble, a thicker one, the bass. Shortening the tailpiece will loosen a tight action; elevating the tailpiece will soften volume and enrich tone. Substituting a non-adjustable bridge whose entire base rests on the guitar will enhance sustaining power.

D'Aquisto is himself an accomplished player and is carefully attuned to the subtler nuances of tone color that his professional clientele seeks. Watching him voice an instrument is a uniquely edifying experience.

He has expanded and developed to a remarkable degree the legacy of skill bequeathed by his old teacher, John D'Angelico. In his grasp of the manifold aspects of guitar making, D'Aquisto is a unique figure. The standard he has set for arched-top guitars will be hard to match.

BIBLIOGRAPHY

Alton, Robert. *Violin and Cello Building and Repairing*. London: Cassell, 1950.

Baines, Anthony. *Musical Instruments Through the Ages*. Baltimore, Md.: Penguin Books, 1961.

Behlen, H., & Bro., Inc. *The Art of Wood Finishing*. New York: H. Behlen & Bro., Inc., 1957.

Bellson, Julius. *The Gibson Story*. Kalamazoo, Mich.: Gibson Inc. 1973.

Dolge, Alfred. *Pianos and Their Makers*. New York: Dover, 1972.

Helmholtz, Hermann. *The Sensations of Tone*. New York: Dover, 1954.

Heron-Allen, ed. *Violin-Making*. London: Ward Lock Ltd., 1884.

Hill, W. Henry. *Antonio Stradivari*. New York: Dover, 1963.

Hofmeister, Theodorus, Jr. "Torres, the Creator of the Modern Guitar." *Guitar Review*, no. 16 (1954).

Hubbard, Frank. *Three Centuries of Harpsichord Making*. Cambridge, Mass.: Harvard University Press, 1965.

Huttig, H. E., II. "The Guitar Maker and His Techniques." *Guitar Review*, no. 28 (1965).

Jones, Hempstock, Mulholland, Stott. *Acoustics*. London: English Universities Press Ltd., 1967.

Longworth, Mike. *Martin Guitars, A History*. Cedar Knolls, N. J.: Colonial Press, 1975.

Mackley, George E. *Wood Engraving*. London: National Magazine Company, 1948.

Turnbull, Harvey. *The Guitar*. London: B. T. Batsford Ltd., 1974.

Wheeler, Tom. *The Guitar Book*. New York: Harper & Row, 1974.

Wood Handbook, U. S. Department of Agriculture, U. S. Government Printing Office, Washington, D. C. 20402.

Periodicals

Guitar Review, 409 E. 50th Street, New York, New York 10022. Handsome magazine devoted to all aspects of the classic guitar.

Guild of American Luthiers Newsletter, 8222 South Park Avenue, Tacoma, Washington 98408. Chatty, informal forum for instrument building lore.

Pickin', Universal Graphics Corp., 1 Saddle Road, Cedar Knolls, New Jersey 07927. Bluegrass and Country music with occasional articles of interest to luthiers.

SUPPLY SOURCES

A. Constantine & Son, Inc.
2050 Eastchester Road, Bronx, New York 10461
Supplies, wood, veneers, tools. Catalog.

Vitali Import Co.
5944-48 Atlantic Boulevard, Maywood,
    California 90270
Wood, machines, accessories. Catalog.

Metropolitan Music Co.
160 Tillman Street, Westwood, New Jersey 07675
Wood, tools, supplies (dist. Ibex Tools). Catalog.

Woodcraft Supply Corp.
313 Montvale Avenue, Woburn,
    Massachusetts 01801
Highest quality woodworking tools.

Marina Music
1892 Union Street, San Francisco,
    California 94123
Wood, tools, accessories. Catalog.

International Violin Supply Co.
414 East Baltimore Street, Baltimore,
    Maryland 21202
Wood, varnish, accessories. Catalog.

J. F. Wallo
1319 "F" Street N. W., Washington, D. C.
Wood, tools, supplies. Catalog.

Allied Traders of Miami
P. O. Box 560603 Kendall Branch, Miami,
    Florida 33156
Wood, supplies, accessories. Catalog.

Euphonon Company
P. O. Box 100, Orford, New Hampshire 03777
Wood, supplies, accessories. Catalog.

Paul H. Gesswein & Co., Inc.
235 Park Avenue South, New York, New York 10003
Jeweler's and engraver's supplies. Catalog
(refundable $1). Minimum order $10.

Brookstone Company
Peterborough, New Hampshire 03458
General and hard-to-find tools. Catalog.

H. Behlen & Bro. Inc.
Box 698, Amsterdam, New York 12010
All wood finishing materials. Catalog.
Minimum order $20.

Vera's Art Box
752A Frederick Road, Catonsville, Maryland 21228
Ivory saddles, nuts, odd-size pieces for inlay. Catalog.

John L. Rie, div. Cresthill Industries Inc.
196 Ashburton Avenue, Yonkers, New York 10701
Mother-of-pearl and abalone.
Catalog (refundable $1).
Minimum order $20.

Scott E. Antes
Boulder Junction, Inc., P.O. Box 471
13443 Cleveland Ave., Uniontown, Ohio 44685
Expertly drawn, full-size blueprints of guitars,
banjos, dulcimers and others. Catalog.

CANADA

Bill Lewis Music Ltd.
3607 West Broadway, Vancouver 8, British Columbia
Wood, tools, supplies. Catalog.

ENGLAND

Sidney Evans Ltd.
49 Berkley Street, Birmingham, B1 2LG, England
Wood, tools, supplies. Catalog.

AUSTRALIA

Perfectus Airscrew
175 Mason Street, Newport, 3015 Victoria
Wood.

Lamberti Bros.
366 Victoria Street, North Melbourne, 3061 Victoria
Fret wire, machines.